ST... ...UIDE

# OCR    AS    UNIT G671

CITY OF
LEARNING
CENTRE
SUNDERLAND COLLEGE

# Sociology

## Exploring Socialisation, Culture and Identity

Steve Chapman

D1589507

Philip Allan Updates, an imprint of Hodder Education, part of Hachette UK, Market Place, Deddington, Oxfordshire OX15 OSE

*Orders*

Bookpoint Ltd, 130 Milton Park, Abingdon, Oxfordshire, OX14 4SB

tel: 01235 827720

fax: 01235 400454

e-mail: uk.orders@bookpoint.co.uk

Lines are open 9.00 a.m.–5.00 p.m., Monday to Saturday, with a 24-hour message answering service. You can also order through the Philip Allan Updates website: www.philipallan.co.uk

© Philip Allan Updates 2008

ISBN 978-0-340-96674-7

First printed 2008

Impression number 5 4 3 2

Year 2013 2012 2011 2010 2009

This guide has been written specifically to support students preparing for the OCR AS Sociology Unit G671 examination. The content has been neither approved nor endorsed by OCR and remains the sole responsibility of the author.

Typeset by Phoenix Photosetting, Chatham, Kent

Printed by MPG Books, Bodmin

Hachette UK's policy is to use papers that are natural, renewable and recyclable products and made from wood grown in sustainable forests. The logging and manufacturing processes are expected to conform to the environmental regulations of the country of origin.

P01285

# Contents

## Introduction

■ ■ ■

## Content Guidance

■ ■ ■

## Questions and Answers

# Introduction

This unit guide is for students following the OCR AS Sociology specification. It deals with the unit topic G671 **Exploring Socialisation, Culture and Identity**. This topic is designed to give you a basic introduction to sociological theories aimed at under-standing human behaviour. It focuses on how culture is formed, the role of primary and secondary agents of socialisation and identity formation in relation to gender, ethnicity, age and social class.

There are three sections to this guide:

**Introduction** — this provides advice on how to use this unit guide, an explanation of the skills required in AS sociology and suggestions for effective revision. It concludes with guidance on how to best respond to the unit question paper.

**Content Guidance** — this provides an outline of what is included in the specification for Exploring Socialisation, Culture and Identity. It is designed to make you aware of what you should know before you complete the unit question paper.

**Questions and Answers** — this provides mock exam questions on Exploring Socialisation, Culture and Identity for you to try, together with some sample answers at grade-A and grade-C level. Examiner's comments are included on how the marks are awarded.

# How to use this guide

To use this guide to your best advantage, you should refer to the Introduction and Content Guidance sections from the beginning of your study of Exploring Socialisation, Culture and Identity. However, in order to get full advantage from the Question and Answer section, you would be advised to wait until you have completed your study of the topic, as the questions are wide-ranging. When you are ready to use this section, you should take each question in turn, study it carefully, and either write a full answer yourself or, at the very least, answer parts (a) and (b) fully and write a plan for parts (c) and (d). When you have done this, study the grade-A candidate's answer and compare it with your own, paying close attention to the examiner's comments. You could also look at the grade-C answers and, using the examiner's comments as a guide, work out how to rewrite them to gain higher marks.

These tasks are quite intensive and time-consuming, and you are advised not to try to tackle all the questions at once or in a short space of time. It is better to focus on one at a time, and spread the workload over several weeks — you can always find some time to do this, even while studying another topic. In addition to using the questions to consolidate your own knowledge and develop your exam skills, you should use at least some of the questions as revision practice — even just reading through the grade-A candidates' answers should provide you with useful revision material.

# The AS specification

The aims of the OCR AS Sociology specification are to encourage you to:
- acquire knowledge and a critical understanding of contemporary social processes and social changes
- appreciate the significance of theoretical and conceptual issues in sociological debate
- understand and evaluate sociological methodology and a range of research methods through active involvement in the research process
- develop skills that enable you to focus on your personal identity, roles and responsibilities within society
- develop a lifelong interest in social issues

# Examinable skills

This unit makes up 50% of the marks available for OCR AS Sociology. There are three main examinable skills in the AS specifications, divided into two **Assessment Objectives.**

## Assessment Objective 1

Assessment Objective 1 (AO1) is **knowledge and understanding**; it accounts for 52% of the total AS marks for this unit. After studying AS sociology, you should be able to demonstrate knowledge and understanding of sociological theory, concepts, methods and different types of evidence, especially empirical studies.

At this level, you need to demonstrate some introductory knowledge of theory. It is also a good idea to know some sociological studies, because these often count as evidence in support of a particular view. Conceptual confidence is also important — you should be able to demonstrate that you understand important concepts and apply them when constructing a sociological argument. Generally, you will need to show in a clear and effective manner how theory, concepts, evidence and methods are interlinked, and how they relate to both social life and social problems.

It is important that your acquisition of knowledge and demonstration of understanding go beyond learning by rote. Generally you can achieve this by learning and using knowledge and evidence that is appropriate and relevant to the question set. A good way of doing this is to ask yourself the following questions:
- Do I know the main arguments in the area I am studying?
- Do I know the main sociologists who have contributed to debate in this area?

- Do I understand the concepts used by these sociologists?
- Do I know the empirical studies and data that can be used as evidence to support or undermine particular sociological arguments?

## Assessment Objective 2

Assessment Objective 2 (AO2) is **analysis, evaluation and application**; it is worth 48% of the total AS marks. Analysis and application essentially involve showing the ability to select and analyse different types of evidence and data. In particular, you need to apply and link sociological evidence to specific sociological arguments. You also need to interpret quantitative and qualitative data, i.e. to work out what the data are saying and/or to put them into your own words. It is useful to ask yourself the following questions when working out whether you have acquired this skill:
- What knowledge in the form of studies, concepts etc. is relevant when addressing a particular debate?
- Can I distinguish between facts and opinions?
- Am I capable of identifying patterns and trends in sociological data and uncovering hidden meanings?
- Am I addressing the question throughout the response?
- Am I using the data and information the examiners have given me to full effect?
- Have I applied contemporary issues and debates to the question?
- What evidence in the form of sociological studies and statistical data can I use to support or criticise particular arguments?

Evaluation normally involves assessing the validity of particular sociological arguments and available evidence and data, or critically examining the reliability of the methods used to collect that evidence. The skill of evaluation is an important one and should be applied to all the material you come across during your study of the topic. It is useful to ask yourself the following questions when practising this skill:
- How many sides to the debate can be identified in this area?
- How was the evidence gathered?
- Can the evidence be checked?
- Is there any other evidence relating to this?
- Is the research relevant to contemporary society?
- Who does not agree with this view and why?
- Which evidence and arguments are most convincing and why?
- What have they got to gain from saying that?
- Are class, gender and ethnicity taken into account?

In more practical terms, evaluation means that whenever you are introduced to a sociological theory or study, you should find and learn at least two criticisms that have been made of it. You should also note, of course, which group or person has made these criticisms, as this is an important piece of information.

## AS performance descriptions for sociology

OCR publishes performance descriptions for the A/B boundary and the E/U boundary, which give some insight into what standards of performance are expected to achieve these grades. For the A/B boundary, you are expected to demonstrate accurate knowledge and understanding of a range of sociological theories, methods and concepts, supported by evidence. Appropriate material must be presented in a logical, accurate and coherent manner with few errors of grammar, punctuation and spelling. You also need to demonstrate an ability to select, apply and interpret accurately and appropriately different types of sociological evidence from a range of sources. Finally, you need to analyse and evaluate relevant evidence and arguments.

For the E/U boundary, you need to demonstrate a basic knowledge and understanding of sociological theories, methods and concepts with limited evidence. Candidates characteristically present little sociological material — they often use common sense or anecdotes instead — with limited coherence. Work is often presented with errors of grammar, punctuation and spelling. Moreover, candidates demonstrate a limited ability to select, apply and interpret different types of sociological evidence. Generally, such candidates are also limited in their analysis of sociological materials and in their evaluation of relevant sociological arguments and evidence.

# Study skills and revision strategies

Good preparation for revision starts the minute you begin to study sociology. One of the most important revision aids that you will have is your sociology folder, so it is important that you keep this in good order. Essentially, it should be divided into topic areas. It should contain all your class notes, handouts, notes you have made from textbooks, class and homework exercises and, of course, all your marked and returned work. If you are not by nature a neat and tidy person, you may find that you have to rewrite notes you make in class into a legible and coherent form before putting them in your folder. Be warned, though — this is something you should do straight away, as even after only a few days you will have forgotten things. If you keep a good folder throughout, reading through this will form a major part of your revision. In addition, you will, of course, need to re-read the relevant parts of your textbooks. Your own work also forms an important revision resource. Go back over your essays and exam answers, read your teacher's comments, and use these to see whether you can redo any pieces that did not score particularly good marks.

You should always write down the definition of a concept when you first come across it — it is a good idea to use a separate part of your folder for this purpose. In addition, it is useful to make a brief summary of research studies, particularly those not found in your textbook. Remember to include the title, author(s) and, most importantly, the date along with your summary of the method(s) used and the main findings. These should be kept in a section in your sociology folder, or you may wish to use a set of index cards for this purpose.

Another important aspect of revision is to practise writing answers within the appropriate time limit. Make sure you have sufficient time not only to complete all the parts of the question, but also to re-read your answer, in order to correct any silly mistakes that may have crept in while working under pressure.

Finally, you need to ensure that you have a thorough understanding of a range of appropriate concepts and studies. Again, this planned and comprehensive revision is not something that can be done the night before the exam — you should start at least a couple of weeks before the exam and revise in concentrated bursts of time. For most people, two or three stints of an hour at a time spread out over a day or two will be more productive than a single 2- or 3-hour session.

# The unit question paper

Exploring Socialisation, Culture and Identity is the only unit G671 topic, and the unit examination will contain only **one** data-response question. You will have 90 minutes to answer this. The unit is worth 50% of the AS marks and 25% of the full A-level. The question totals 100 marks, composed of 52 marks for AO1 (knowledge and understanding) and 48 marks for AO2. AO2 marks are made up of 24 marks for interpretation (AO2(a)) and 24 marks for evaluation and analysis (AO2(b)).

Approximately 8 weeks before the examination, you will be given one item of pre-release material of approximately 1,000 words of sociological research focused on some aspect of identity. This is likely to describe the aims and context of the research as well as the methodology and sampling techniques used. There will also be some reference to the research findings. You should examine and analyse this pre-release material carefully because it will form the main part of your response to the part (d) section of the examination paper. It may also offer you some information that could be used to illustrate sociological points in other parts of the examination paper, notably part (c).

The examination question is divided into parts 1–4, worth 100 marks in total. Question 1, which is worth 8 marks for AO1 'knowledge and understanding', will ask you to define a concept central to Exploring Socialisation, Culture and Identity and to illustrate with examples. Try to avoid using commonsense or anecdotal examples. Wherever possible, use sociological studies, theories or facts. It is recommended that you spend 5 minutes at most on this question, and write a brief but detailed paragraph.

Question 2 will ask you to 'outline and explain how' two influences shape identity. The question is worth 16 marks — divided into 12 AO1 marks for 'knowledge and understanding' and 4 AO2 (a) marks for 'interpretation and application'. It is likely that this question will focus on 'socialisation', so you should be aware of how different agencies of socialisation create and reinforce different aspects of identity. The examiner expects to see the use of empirical sociological studies in support of your explanation, as well as confident use of sociological concepts. It is recommended that you spend 15 minutes at most on this question and write about half a side of A4.

Question 3 will ask you to 'explain and briefly evaluate' some aspect of identity and how it relates to recent social change. The question is worth 24 marks — divided into 12 AO1 marks for 'knowledge and understanding', 8 AO2 (a) marks for 'interpretation and application' and 4 AO2 (b) marks for 'evaluation and analysis'. With regard to 'knowledge and understanding', the examiner expects to see detailed, i.e. 'very good', knowledge of concepts and reasons why particular identities have been adopted by particular social groups. With regard to 'interpretation and application' skills, you must make detailed use of sociological evidence and acknowledge the names of sociologists involved in that research. You can also use studies mentioned in the pre-release material. With regard to 'evaluation and analysis', you need to show awareness of the strengths and weaknesses of such studies. It is recommended that you spend 25 minutes at most on this question and attempt to write at least a side of A4.

Question 4 will ask you to use the pre-release material as the major source of your response, as well as 'your wider sociological knowledge' to 'explain and evaluate the use of' particular research methods mentioned in the pre-release material. This question is worth 52 marks — divided into 20 marks for AO1 'knowledge and understanding', 12 marks for AO2(a) 'interpretation and application' and 20 marks for AO2(b) 'evaluation and analysis'.

As stated earlier, you will have sight of this pre-release material approximately 8 weeks before the examination. You should take full advantage of this opportunity to analyse the research in-depth. This will allow you to work out what methods were used, the sampling frame and techniques that were utilised and the probable strengths and weaknesses of the research.

For 'knowledge and understanding', you are expected to show a 'very good' knowledge and understanding of the methods used in the study contained in the pre-release material. You will need to know in detail the advantages of using a method(s) and how these relate to the concepts of reliability, validity, representativeness and generalisability. You should also be able to make brief reference to the sociological theories of positivism and interpretivism.

With regard to 'interpretation and application', the examiner expects you to explain and justify the choice of research methods and sampling technique with reference to practical, theoretical and ethical reasons. You should use examples from the pre-release materials and your wider sociological knowledge, i.e. what you have revised, to illustrate these reasons.

For 'evaluation and analysis', you will need to consider the potential disadvantages or weaknesses of using the methods and sampling technique mentioned in the

pre-release material, with reference to concepts such as reliability, validity, repre-sentativeness and generalisability. Again, you should use examples from the pre-release material and from your revision knowledge to illustrate these points.

# Content Guidance

This section is intended to show you the major issues and themes covered in Exploring Socialisation, Culture and Identity. However, it does not provide an exhaustive or comprehensive list of the concepts, issues and sociological studies that you could use to answer questions on this topic. Rather, it is an outline guide that should give you a good idea of the key concepts and some issues and sociological studies that are worth further investigation. You should be able to access further useful information from your teacher, the textbook you are using and past copies of *Sociology Review*.

The content of Exploring Socialisation, Culture and Identity falls into eight main areas:
- the formation of culture
- the process of socialisation
- the role of socialisation in the creation of gender identities
- the role of socialisation in the creation of social-class identities
- the role of socialisation in the creation of ethnic identities
- the role of socialisation in the creation of age identities
- exploring the research process
- research methods

The topic is designed to give you an introduction to key concepts associated with developing a sociological understanding of the contemporary social world. Hopefully you will achieve a good understanding of the relationship between individuals and social structures. In particular, this topic aims to examine influences such as gender, social class, ethnicity, religion and age on people's sense of identity and their social behaviour — in short, how and to what extent social forces shape people. You will also be expected to acquire an overview of how agencies of socialisation — the family, education, media, religion, the peer group and workplace — work in practice, in terms of how they socialise individuals and groups into a sense of identity.

With regard to the research process, you need to be aware of the main stages of social research and the main principles of research design. You will be expected to have an overview of the main quantitative and qualitative methods of data collection and to be able to assess their strengths and weaknesses in terms of reliability, validity and the subjects that they may be suitable for researching. You will also need to be able to differentiate between quantitative and qualitative forms of data and to interpret and analyse such data.

content guidance

# The formation of culture

- A society is a social group that normally occupies a given geographical territory and shares a sense of belonging to a common culture and set of institutions.
- Culture refers to the way of life of a social group or society. Individuals who share beliefs, values, norms, rituals, language, history and knowledge generally conform to a similar cultural outlook.
- UK society is characterised by cultural diversity — its culture has fragmented into competing subcultures. Subcultures are social groups based on social class, age, religion and ethnicity that subscribe to the values and norms of mainstream society in most respects but also subscribe to cultural values, norms, customs etc. that are unique to them. Subcultures may be defined as different or deviant by the majority culture (e.g. ethnic minority cultures, youth cultures).
- A multicultural society is one in which cultural diversity is acknowledged and encouraged. Aspects of all cultures — majority and minority — are accepted and celebrated. The emphasis in multicultural societies is on all ethnic subcultures living alongside each other peacefully and respecting one another's beliefs and customs.
- High culture is a controversial concept, suggesting that some cultural creations should have the highest status because they represent the highest levels of human creativity and are superior to other cultural products and leisure activities. Forms of high culture include classical music, opera, ballet, art in the form of traditional paintings and sculpture, Shakespeare, great literature and poetry. High culture is an important part of the identity of the economic and political elite, i.e. the upper class, in the UK.
- Mass or popular culture refers to the products of the mass media in modern capitalist societies such as television programmes, films, popular fiction, magazines, comics and popular music. Some sociologists have argued that this type of culture is manufactured for mass consumption rather than created for its own sake, and consequently, it has little or no artistic merit compared with the products of high culture.
- Consumer culture refers to the emphasis put on consumerism (i.e. advertising) and consumption (i.e. shopping/buying) and materialism in modern capitalist societies. Some sociologists argue that a by-product of this type of society is 'conspicuous consumption' — people's identity and status today is acquired through the purchase and consumption of designer labels and other high-status goods and activities.
- The concept of global culture refers to the increasing trend for local cultures to be influenced by the values, norms, fashions, tastes etc. of other cultures, particularly US culture. For example, the culture of the UK in 1958 was largely shaped by home-grown influences — although there was some American influence over their choice of music or films, British people mainly enjoyed British food such as roast beef and Yorkshire pudding or fish and chips, and shopped in specifically

British outlets such as Marks and Spencer, W.H. Smith and Boots. They watched mainly British television programmes and dressed in clothes largely manufactured in the UK. In 2008, British culture has been influenced by globalisation, and consequently we are just as likely to enjoy Chinese, Italian, Indian and American fast food as we are to enjoy British food. We drink continental lagers and wines, and celebrate popular events such as Halloween and Mother's Day, which originated in the USA.

# Values and norms

- Values are beliefs and goals relating to what members of a society or culture feel is morally important and desirable; they act as general guidelines for behaviour.
- The principal values of UK culture include respect for human life, free speech, achievement, equality of opportunity, materialism, individualism and privacy.
- Norms are the cultural expectations that societies attach to particular types of behaviour on the basis of sharing key values. For example, the belief in privacy means that people generally do not pry into the intimate affairs of others and do not read one another's mail or diaries.
- Customs are norms that have been established in a society for generations and are usually part of the historical traditions of a society that mark it out as culturally unique and distinctive, e.g. in the UK this might be Bonfire Night, and in Wales it might be St David's Day.

# Roles and status

- Social roles are sets of norms that are culturally expected of individuals. For example, the role of mother in the contemporary UK involves expectations about how 'good' mothers should behave, and is consequently used by society to judge individuals who do not live up to these expectations.
- Status refers to the prestige attached to a particular role because members of society value highly the behaviour associated with the role. For example, doctors are held in high regard because their behaviour is directly concerned with saving lives.
- In some societies, roles and status may be ascribed, meaning that they are fixed at birth by descent or inheritance, or by physical characteristics such as skin colour or gender. Norms relating to the work people do, relationships, marriage, political and economic power etc. are restricted and often unchangeable.
- In Western societies, roles and status tend to be achieved because members of society value equality of opportunity and meritocracy.
- A meritocratic society is one which rewards people on merit alone and is open to all. All social groups are protected and regulated equally in the eyes of the law.

**Evaluation**

+ Values, norms, roles and statuses are relative to particular historical periods, societies and subcultures, and consequently often change.
- The notion of meritocracy may be exaggerated — there is evidence that some subcultures in the UK, particularly the working class and some ethnic minority groups, are regarded as 'inferior' by powerful groups. They may consequently be discriminated against and find it difficult to achieve the roles and status achieved by other groups.

**Key concepts**

society; culture; cultural diversity; subcultures; values; norms; role; customs; ascribed status; achieved status; meritocracy, multiculturalism; globalisation; consumerism; consumption; materialism; high culture; popular culture

# The process of socialisation

Socialisation is the learning of cultural attitudes and behaviour. Studies of feral children demonstrate the importance of the socialisation process, because children who lack sustained contact with other humans lack basic social skills such as language and interpersonal interaction.

There are two broad types of socialisation: primary and secondary socialisation.

# Primary socialisation

Parents and families play the crucial role in primary socialisation. Parents transmit the values and norms necessary for children to demonstrate the social competence required to be accepted socially as good citizens. This process usually results in the development of a conscience and guilt as a child learns the boundaries of acceptable and unacceptable behaviour. Parents also act as role models, and children internalise key values through imitation. Children's sense of identity is therefore shaped by the social reaction of their parents, and partly by culture, because most parents follow dominant cultural norms with regard to child rearing.

# Secondary socialisation

Whereas the principal agents of primary socialisation are parents and families, there are several agents of secondary socialisation.

## The education system

Socialisation in schools involves the transmission of knowledge and skills, and key values such as achievement, individualism and competition are transmitted through setting, sport, assemblies and speech days, for example. The teaching of national identity in literature, language and history may result in a pride in belonging to a wider social group, such as a society or religious organisation.

Consensus (functionalist) sociologists believe that socialisation in schools produces model pupils and citizens. Conflict sociologists (Marxists and feminists) argue that schools operate a hidden curriculum that socialises subordinate social groups into ruling-class and patriarchal culture and the passive acceptance of failure, and therefore inequality.

### Evaluation

– Evidence from studies such as those carried out by Willis or Fuller indicate that pupils can successfully resist the hidden curriculum.
– Not all pupils become model pupils or conformists, as can be seen by the existence of anti-school subcultures, classroom disruption, truancy and exclusion.

## The peer group

A peer group is usually a group of people of similar age who are connected by friendship and/or similar experiences, and who influence one another in terms of behaviour, tastes etc. Peer groups may be organised formally, e.g. at work, in a society or club, or informally, e.g. gangs or deviant youth subcultures.

The values and behaviour of such a group can influence the behaviour of individuals, especially in adolescence. Anti-school, delinquent and deviant subcultures may encourage young people to adopt values and norms in opposition to those of mainstream culture.

Occupational peer groups may shape individual behaviour, e.g. by imposing ethical constraints, influencing attitudes towards employers, supplying people with a strong or weak sense of class identity and stressing that community comes before the individual.

### Evaluation

– Surveys indicate that on most issues, young people are generally in broad agreement with their parents.
– Most youth rebellion is temporary or short-term.

## Religion

Religion is a key agent of socialisation because it socialises people into moral values. These provide the guidelines that underpin other agencies of socialisation, especially the family and education, e.g. disapproval of adultery. The transmission of religious values, especially in ethnic minority cultures, may function to integrate people, i.e. give them a strong sense of belonging to a moral community and identity.

### Evaluation

- The influence of religion as an agent of socialisation may be undermined by the general national decline in religious practice and belief.
- Conflict sociologists argue that religious values are aimed primarily at persuading poor and powerless groups to accept the inevitability of inequalities such as poverty.

## Mass media

The mass media may have replaced religion in importance as a secondary agent of socialisation. Some media sociologists have expressed concern about the influence of media content on the behaviour of young children, e.g. they suggest that violence and anti-social behaviour is increasing because of exposure to violent images on television and film.

Other sociologists are concerned about the socialisation function of the media in reinforcing stereotypes — and therefore prejudice and discrimination — about less powerful social groups, such as women, ethnic minorities, the disabled and homosexuals.

Postmodern sociologists claim that the mass media have socialised people into abandoning traditional sources of identity such as class and gender. The media in modern society socialise people into seeing their identity as shaped by style and conspicuous consumption (e.g. designer labels, fashion, logos, being seen in the right places).

### Evaluation

- There is no compelling evidence that media content has a negative effect on young people's behaviour.
- It is almost impossible to prove that media socialisation shapes people's attitudes and prejudices.
- The view that the media socialise society's members into seeing consumption as more important than class or gender as a source of personal identity is exaggerated.

## The workplace

Our experience at work not only teaches us skills and work discipline, but also the informal rules that underpin work, i.e. the tricks of the trade. We may also be influenced to behave in particular ways by our membership of formal work-based organisations. For example, membership of a trade union may produce a collectivist outlook in which an individual puts the interest of the group before his/her own interests, and membership of a professional organisation such as the Law Society or the British Medical Association will make clear how a professional person should behave in practice.

**Evaluation**

– There is evidence that membership of collectivist organisations such as trade unions is in decline and that workers are adopting more individualist attitudes.

# Socialisation and social control

Socialisation involves social control, i.e. once social rules have been learnt, they need to be frequently enforced through the use of positive and negative sanctions. Social control refers to the means by which society makes sure we adhere to the values and norms that we have learnt during socialisation. Formal agencies of social control include the law, the police and judicial system. Informal agencies of social control include the family, the peer group, the mass media and religion.

Families act as agents of social control over their children. For example, during social-isation, our family teaches us the difference between right and wrong, and develops our conscience. It is argued by New Right sociologists that some families and parents, particularly those belonging to the underclass, socialise their children into a set of deviant values that result in them being anti-authority, work shy and welfare-depen-dent. Feminist sociologists argue that one reason why females are less involved in crime is because they are subjected to greater social controls by their parents than boys are.

Some sociologists argue that the mass media is a social control agency. Functionalists note that, by reporting crime and punishment, the mass media remind us what the rules (laws) of society are. They also define what counts as appropriate behaviour for men and women, young and old etc. For example, a woman who does not conform to media expectations about femininity may find herself defined as deviant, and moral panics may be used by the older generation to control the younger generation. By creating social anxiety about youth groups and behaviour, the tabloid media are able to push for stricter controls through more policing and new laws.

# The consensus approach to socialisation

A debate is going on between sociologists about the function of socialisation. Consensus sociologists argue that all members of society agree on fundamental, or core, values. The function of socialisation is to make sure that all members of society are fully integrated into these common values, and so share a sense of belonging.

The nuclear family is the vital agency of socialisation because it transmits culture from one generation to another, so ensuring the reproduction of society and social order. The family acts as a personality factory, producing children whose behaviour is shaped by key values such as individualism and achievement. Parents benefit because they gain stability and satisfaction from the parenting experience. However, some consensus sociologists argue that socialisation in modern society is becoming less effective because of increasing trends such as divorce and the lack of a father in many one-parent families.

### Evaluation

- The consensus view overestimates the success of the socialisation process, as indicated by the existence of problems such as child abuse, youth suicide and eating disorders.
- So-called common values may be the values of dominant social groups.
- This view presents an 'over-socialised' view of children. For example, children may negotiate socialisation with parents, and parents may be socialised into particular ways of thinking or behaving by their children.
- The consensus approach presents socialisation as a phenomenon which is experienced by everybody in the same way — this neglects differences due to wealth, social class, ethnicity, religion etc.
- There is no universal agreement on how socialisation should occur, as indicated by the debate about smacking children.
- There is evidence from Phoenix, Cashmore and others that one-parent families can socialise children successfully, and the absence of a father does not necessarily damage children.

# The conflict approach to socialisation

Conflict sociologists argue that society is composed of a variety of competing value systems, but some groups have more power than others to impose their values on subordinate groups. For example, the wealthy have more power than the working-class and the poor, men generally have more power than women, and white people usually have more power than ethnic minorities. According to conflict sociologists, the function of socialisation is to make sure that children grow up accepting inequality, hierarchy, exploitation and patriarchy (i.e. male dominance) as natural facts of life. Socialisation is therefore about learning to conform and accepting one's lot.

### Evaluation

- There is little agreement among conflict sociologists about the source of this inequality. Some argue it is social class, others suggest it is status such as race and age, while others argue it is gender.
- This is an over-socialised picture of human beings — it presents socialisation as a one-way process that cannot be resisted or negotiated.
- It presents people as brainwashed cultural dopes with no freedom of choice.

### Key concepts

primary socialisation; secondary socialisation; social control; positive and negative sanctions; conscience; role models; hidden curriculum; peer group; conspicuous consumption; ideology; stereotyping; consensus; core or common values; conflict; power; value consensus; hierarchy; patriarchy

# The role of socialisation in the creation of gender identities

Sex refers to biological differences between males and females; gender refers to the cultural expectations attached to feminine and masculine roles.

Some consensus sociologists believe that gender roles are biologically determined and are therefore fixed and unchangeable. Feminists, however, argue that gender roles are socially constructed in traditional and patriarchal ways via gender role socialisation.

Traditional views of masculinity emphasise that males should be physically active, authoritative, aspirational and in control of their emotions, and that they are more suited to leadership and the breadwinner role than females. Traditional views of femininity emphasise that females are passive, emotional, more concerned with their appearance, more adept at caring and more suited to domestic work than men are. Feminists suggest that these ideas about what constitutes the 'feminine' (i.e. the mother-housewife and sex object) are defined and shaped by men.

## Gender role socialisation

### The family

From an early age, people are trained to conform to social expectations about their gender. Much of this training goes on in the family during primary socialisation.

Oakley (1982) identifies two processes central to the construction of gender identity:
- Manipulation refers to the way in which parents encourage or discourage behaviour on the basis of appropriateness for the child's sex.
- Canalisation refers to the way in which parents channel children's interests into toys and activities that are seen as 'normal for that sex'.

Manipulation and canalisation involve the learning and internalisation of gender role codes through the following aspects of socialisation:
- imitation of parental role models
- parents rewarding gender-appropriate behaviour
- parents discouraging gender-inappropriate behaviour, e.g. crying in boys
- parents adopting different modes of speech depending on the gender of the child

- mothers' preoccupation with female children's appearance
- parents giving children gender-specific toys, books and games
- children being dressed in gender-appropriate clothes and colours
- parents assigning gender-specific household chores to children
- parents socially controlling the behaviour of girls more tightly than that of boys

## Education

Until the 1990s, the hidden curriculum transmitted gender-stereotyped assumptions about feminine behaviour through such things as teacher expectations, timetabling of subject choices, career advice and textbook content. Despite increasing educational success for females in the last 10 years, the persistence of gender differences in subject choices, especially in further and higher education, indicates that this may still be a problem today. In particular, working-class girls are still following traditional gender routes — leaving school at 16, temporary jobs, marriage and motherhood. There is also some evidence that the hidden curriculum through teacher expectations may be resulting in working-class boys following traditional gender routes into manual jobs. Controlling masculine behaviour may become more important than ensuring that boys receive a good education.

Recent studies suggest that young males may reject academic work because their experience of their mothers helping them with homework and the likelihood that their primary school teacher was female means that they equate learning with femininity.

## The peer group

There is evidence that working-class boys may reject the goals of schooling and set up anti-school subcultures organised around deviant activities and the exaggeration of aspects of masculinity, e.g. aggression, toughness and risk taking.

Mac An Ghaill suggests that such subcultures may be a reaction to a 'crisis in masculinity', as working-class boys learn that traditional working-class jobs and roles such as breadwinner and head of household are in decline. Membership of deviant subcultures may confer status on boys who exaggerate masculine values and norms, while punishing behaviour defined as feminine by calling into question the masculine identity of boys who choose academic paths.

## The mass media

Feminists are critical of a range of mass media that socialise females into either domestic or sexualised patterns of femininity:
- Popular literature, especially fairy tales and children's stories, portray females as the weaker sex and males as heroic guardians of female virtue.
- The content of children's books confirms traditional gender roles in terms of the role models offered in them.
- Comics and magazines for teenage adolescents encourage them to concentrate on appearance and romance rather than on education and careers.

- Women's magazines are apprentice manuals for motherhood and domesticity.
- Television, cinema and advertising continue to show women disproportionately in domestic roles or as appendages of successful men, and emphasise their physical looks and sex appeal at the expense of their ability or personality.
- 'New lads' magazines and pornography assert a traditional view of masculinity, organised around interpreting women as sexual objects, sport and drinking culture.

### Evaluation

- The concept of gender role socialisation is over-deterministic and paints an over-socialised picture of children.
- Some males and females may be happy to choose traditional gender roles; as Hakim points out, some women want and enjoy the role of mother and housewife.
- Other studies point out that processes such as the hidden curriculum and the interpretation of media images are not uncritically internalised by children; they are negotiated and perhaps even resisted.
- It is difficult to prove that media images have an effect on gender stereotyping; the family may be a more important agency of socialisation.
- The educational success of females and the feminisation of the workforce suggest that traditional gender role socialisation may not be as powerful as feminists think it is.
- The main victims of gender role socialisation, according to the sociological literature, seem to be working-class boys and girls — does this indicate that class is more important than gender?

# New forms of femininity and masculinity

Sociologists suggest that traditional or hegemonic definitions of masculinity and femininity are in decline. New forms of femininity and masculinity are supposedly emerging.

## New femininities?

Surveys by Sue Sharpe suggest that teenage girls' attitudes are more aspirational today compared with Sharpe's study of teenage girls in 1974, which found that they stressed marriage and motherhood as their main ambitions. Helen Wilkinson argues that females today are radically different in attitude and ambition from previous generations. She refers to this change in attitude towards education and careers as a 'genderquake'. The workforce has become increasingly feminised, thus increasing women's financial and cultural power. For example, women are increasingly the main economic breadwinners in areas characterised by high male unemployment.

Increasing cultural power may be reflected in the increase in women petitioning for divorce (they outnumber men), single-person households and voluntary childlessness. Surveys indicate that women are demanding more power in marriage, expect more out of their husbands and partners, and are no longer willing to put up with abuse or empty-shell marriages. There is some anecdotal evidence for young females adopting masculine values and norms, especially in regard to sex, drinking culture and girl gangs.

## New masculinities?

An increasing number of men are choosing to be househusbands. It is argued that the emergence of a 'new man', who shares childcare and housework, may be a reaction to the crisis in masculinity (the lack of traditional jobs and roles for men is forcing them to change their behaviour). The increasing feminisation of masculinity may be reflected in the advertising and marketing of men's cosmetics and toiletries.

Postmodernists suggest that men and women now see consumption and leisure as the key factors in defining and shaping their identity, rather than masculinity and femininity.

### Evaluation

- Change may be exaggerated — the evidence suggests that patriarchy is still influential, as reflected in the lack of women in top jobs and the 18% pay gap between men and women.
- Many women who work still have the dual burden of being mainly responsible for housework and childcare.
- There is a tendency in accounts of gender role socialisation to treat men's and women's experiences as the same and to ignore class and ethnic differences in experience. It is unlikely, for example, that Asian or working-class women experience these changes to the same degree as middle-class white women.
- Men dominate consumption of leisure because they have more economic power than women and more free time.
- Men may be reacting to the crisis in masculinity in traditional ways, i.e. by turning in frustration to violence, sexism, crime and anti-subcultures based on exaggerating masculine values.

### Key concepts

gender role socialisation; femininity; masculinity; manipulation; canalisation; crisis in masculinity; deviant subcultures; sexual objects; genderquake; feminisation of the workforce; hegemonic masculinity; voluntary childlessness; the new man; the feminisation of masculinity; consumption

# The role of socialisation in the creation of social-class identities

Our identity is strongly bound up with our employment and workplace, and the income, status and lifestyle that arise out of it. There is evidence that class identity, which is based on the job we do and the income (wage or salary) we receive, is a powerful influence on the social relationships we forge. For example, workplace peer groups are often the basis of social networks outside work. Generally, it is agreed that three broad social class groupings exist in the UK: the upper class, the middle classes and the working class.

## The upper class

This group is defined by its wealth rather than occupation. Many members of this class have inherited wealth and consequently do not need to work for a salary or wage.

A key value of this group is that economic power (wealth) is a source of opportunity, privilege and power over others, which is worth reproducing and protecting. Upper-class families share common social backgrounds because of intermarriage and extended kinship networks, which are largely closed to outsiders. Children from such backgrounds are socialised into a culture of privilege by their parents, organised around common attitudes, language and exclusive social pursuits.

An important part of the socialisation of upper-class children is their schooling, which takes place mainly in exclusive and expensive private schools (public schools), e.g. Eton, Harrow, Winchester. Such schools socialise upper-class children into the values of conservatism, respect for tradition, nationalism and acceptance of authority and hierarchy as natural outcomes of superior breeding and upbringing. Public school students are encouraged to see themselves as an elite. The peer group is central because it functions outside schools as an old-boy network in adulthood, which confers economic and cultural advantages on its members.

## The middle classes

Sociologists largely agree that the middle classes are defined by their non-manual work. They can be divided into a number of distinct class fractions (e.g. professionals, managers, the self-employed and white-collar workers) that differ in terms of economic rewards, lifestyle and cultural attitudes. According to Light, these fractions share some common suburban values, including the need to communicate social position through conspicuous consumption, home ownership, resistance to social change, respectability and decency, and a sense of social difference.

Evidence suggests that the middle-class family is more child-centred than families in the other two social groups. This benefits middle-class children in particular in secondary, further and higher education. Parents have economic capital that can be spent on educational toys, books and technology, private tuition and homes in areas with good schools. They can also pass on 'cultural capital' — values, beliefs, knowledge and language skills, which benefit children in educational environments. Moreover, middle-class parents can use their 'social capital' to benefit their children — they have the confidence, communication skills and contacts to get the most out of education for their children.

Savage notes differences between the middle-class fractions of professionals and managers in terms of cultural attitudes and pursuits, e.g. professionals are more likely to take an interest in the arts than managers. Saunders notes differences in the cultural values of privately employed professionals and those employed by the state, e.g. the former tend to be highly individualistic, while the latter tend to be more community-orientated.

Marxists such as Braverman argue that white-collar workers are experiencing radical changes in the workplace due to technology, restructuring and the introduction of working practices such as those found in call centres. This has resulted in the deskilling of such workers, which, according to Braverman, has led to a reduction in pay, living standards and status. He suggests that they have experienced 'proletarianisation' — they have become similar to the working class in terms of their economic lifestyles and consequently their cultural outlooks.

### Evaluation

- A lack of empirical research may mean that generalisations are being made about middle-class culture.
- Marshall's survey of class attitudes found that 50% of his white-collar sample saw themselves as working class, but their attitudes and lifestyle differed considerably from those of manual workers.

# The working class

Until the late twentieth century, many working-class manual workers subscribed to a 'proletarian traditionalist' identity that had the following characteristics:
- They lived in tight-knit communities, close to their place of work, e.g. mining communities.
- They saw society in terms of 'them' versus 'us', (i.e. workers versus bosses) and consequently had a strong awareness of and pride in their class position.

- The extended family — parents and children, grandparents, cousins etc. — were important because they acted as a mutual support system offering economic, social and emotional supports.
- They had a strong sense of loyalty to their occupational peer group. This community was demonstrated in their membership of trade unions and working men's clubs, as well as their tendency to vote for the Labour Party, which was traditionally seen as the party that best represented the interests of manual workers.

Some sociologists also identified a 'deferential working class' composed of rural manual workers, whose value system stressed traditional attitudes and beliefs, e.g. respect for their employers, voting for the Conservative Party.

# Changes in working-class identity

Since the 1960s, there has been a major decline in manual work and the number of proletarian traditionalist workers, as traditional industries such as mining, shipbuilding, iron and steel and factory work have gone into recession. Consequently, the proletarian traditionalist identity is less common. Some sociologists argue that a new type of working-class identity has become dominant, starting in the latter part of the twentieth century. This is known as the instrumental and privatised working class, because the workers who are part of it supposedly no longer see their class as important. Instead, they define themselves through their families and they work purely for instrumental reasons (i.e. for money) in order to improve their privatised lives (i.e. their homes and standard of living).

These sociologists also argue that the high unemployment of the 1980s and 1990s has led to the emergence of an underclass characterised by an anti-work, welfare-dependent and crime-prone culture.

Some postmodernist commentators believe that working-class identity is in terminal decline, because people now judge each other on the basis of consumption of style and labels rather than on the basis of social class.

### Evaluation

- A lack of recent empirical research may mean that generalisations are being made about working-class culture.
- Studies of the poor and long-term unemployed suggest that they subscribe to the same ideas about work, family and crime as everyone else.
- Charlesworth's research in Rotherham, South Yorkshire, indicates that the poor do not voluntarily choose to be welfare dependent. Their situation is caused by social factors beyond their control such as recession, globalisation and government policies.
- Marshall's survey indicates that manual workers still see social class as very important.

**Key concepts**

employment situation; market situation; culture of privilege; old-boy network; class fractions; suburban identity; cultural capital; deskilling; proletarianisation; proletarian traditionalist; deferential worker; instrumental collectivist; mutual support system; extended kin; underclass; welfare dependency

# The role of socialisation in the creation of ethnic identities

In the UK, the term 'ethnic minority' generally refers to people who originated in the former British colonies of the Indian subcontinent and the Caribbean. It implies 'alien' or 'immigrant', yet the majority of people of ethnic minority extraction living in the UK are British-born and hold British nationality.

**Evaluation**

- The use of the term 'ethnic minority' neglects the fact that many ethnic minorities are white.
- The use of the term 'ethnic minorities' ignores the fact that members of these groups have very different geographical roots, histories, religions, traditions and lifestyles.
- The term 'ethnic minority', along with 'white' and 'black', disguises differences based on social class and gender.

## The meaning of ethnic identity

A number of cultural characteristics distinguish ethnic minority cultures in the UK:

- Their members share common descent — especially racial origin and skin colour.
- Their members share geographical origin or roots.
- Their members share the same language, in addition to English.
- Their members share a common historical experience.
- Their religion is likely to be non-Christian; or if it is Christian, it may involve a form of worship different from that experienced by the majority culture.
- Customs may mean that dress codes, family life, food and food preparation, music, ceremonies etc. may be interpreted as 'exotic' by the majority population.

# Agents of ethnic minority socialisation

## The family

The family is the central source of identity for Indian, Pakistani and Bangladeshi people. Hill found that family commitments lay at the heart of Asian communities in Leicester.

Ghumann (1999) outlined some of the family or primary socialisation practices found in many Asian families:

- Children are brought up to be obedient, loyal to and respectful of their elders and community.
- Arranged marriage, based on negotiation with one's parents, is generally accepted by the majority of young people.
- Respect for religion is still considered to be important, particularly in Muslim families.
- The mother tongue is seen as crucial in maintaining links between generations and in the transmission of religious values. Children therefore tend to be bilingual, and are often able to use the mother language (e.g. Urdu, Punjabi, Gujerati and Hindi) and English interchangeably.
- There is a strong sense of obligation to the elderly and extended kin.

## Education

Studies of ethnic minority experience of education have focused on the hidden curriculum:

- Studies of hidden curriculum content suggest that ethnic minority culture, history and religion are rendered invisible or less important than white culture.
- Studies of teacher expectations indicate that teachers may label African-Caribbean culture as a problem because its values are seen to be in conflict with school culture.
- Studies by Troyna, Mac An Ghaill and Fuller indicate that some students may exaggerate aspects of African-Caribbean culture to resist racial stereotyping in schools, usually via anti-school subcultures.
- Studies of Indian children indicate the importance of educational success to family identity.

## Religion

For some ethnic minority groups, particularly Indian, Pakistani, Bangladeshi and Jewish groups, religion is probably the most influential agent of socialisation outside the family.

Jacobson notes that young Pakistanis see being Muslim as more important than being Pakistani or British. Islam has a strong impact on young Pakistani and Bangladeshi identity in terms of their diet, worship, dress, behaviour and everyday routines and practices. Gardner and Shukur see Islam as compensating for the racism experienced by ethnic minority groups on an everyday basis.

## The peer group

African-Caribbeans may use gangsta rap and hip-hop as a means of coping with the racism and deprivation of everyday urban existence. They may assert black pride and history through urban protest such as riots.

Tony Sewell argues that the male identity of African-Caribbean teenagers is focused on being hyper-male and gangsta in the eyes of their peers. This often compensates for the lack of a father figure in the lives of many of these teenagers, i.e. many live in one-parent families headed by their mothers. Furthermore, Sewell notes that this street identity is shaped partly by media agencies such as advertising and MTV, which encourage young African-Caribbean males to subscribe to a consumer culture that views material items such as clothing, trainers and jewellery (i.e. 'bling') as more important than education.

According to Sewell, the identity of black youth is the result of a 'triple quandary':
- First, they feel rejected by mainstream culture, which is dominated by whites.
- Second, they become anxious about how they are perceived by society, and especially by their black peers. They do not have fathers to turn to for advice or guidance, so they compensate for this anxiety by constructing a deviant and highly masculine identity which stresses being ultra-confident and challenging authority.
- Third, many aspects of this identity are taken from media culture, particularly the emphasis on designer labels and the imitation of male role models, e.g. rap stars, in terms of macho attitudes and forms of behaviour.

This culture of hyper-masculinity is valued as a comfort zone, i.e. their peer group's acceptance of this identity compensates for the strong sense of rejection they feel because of the absence of their fathers, the way the education system treats them and racism from white society.

## White culture

The reaction of the white majority culture to ethnic minority culture is an important influence on socialisation. Surveys suggest that one third of the British population admits to being racially prejudiced. The ways in which ethnic minorities exert their identity may therefore be a reaction to prejudice and discrimination. For example, Modood (1997) found that many African-Caribbeans stress their skin colour as an important source of identity because of their experience of racism. Black pride and power may be celebrated if black youth perceives itself to be excluded deliberately from jobs or stereotyped by white people, especially by symbols of white authority such as teachers and the police.

# Ethnic minority culture: potential change

A lack of empirical evidence characterises this area, but several sociological observations can be made.

There are increasing tensions in some parts of the UK as young Asians, especially Muslims, assert their religious identity, usually in defensive reaction to racist actions. There are increasing tensions between different ethnic minority groups, e.g. African-Caribbeans and Muslims, who rarely mix socially.

There may be generational conflict between ethnic minority parents and children, as the latter come into contact with their white peers and want to adopt Western values with regard to education and marriage. Butler found that young Islamic women subscribed to different identities from their mothers in terms of equality, domestic roles, fashion and marriage. In her study of Chinese restaurants in the UK, Song noted generational tensions in Chinese families as children seek education rather than employment in the family restaurant. This resulted in some Chinese parents viewing their children as 'less Chinese', because they were perceived to be failing to pass on family traditions.

Mixed marriages and relationships between African-Caribbeans and whites continue to increase, e.g. 50% of black men have white partners.

There is some evidence that ethnic identities are evolving and modern hybrid or dual forms of identity are developing among Britain's younger minority ethnic citizens. Charlotte Butler (1995) studied third-generation young British Muslim women (their parents and grandparents were born in Britain), and found that they chose from a variety of possible identities. Some chose to reflect their ascribed position through the wearing of traditional dress, while others took a more 'negotiated' position, e.g. adopting Western ideas about education and careers while retaining some respect for traditional religious ideas about the role of women.

Johal (1998) focused on second- and third-generation British Asians. He found that they have a dual identity, e.g. they inherit an Asian identity and adopt a British one. This results in Asian youth adopting a 'white mask' in order to interact with white peers at school or college, but emphasising their cultural difference whenever they feel it is necessary. He noted that many British Asians adopt 'hybrid identities', defined by Jill Swale as a 'pick-and-mix approach to cultural behaviour patterns found in postmodern societies'. This involves the young selecting aspects of British, Asian and international culture relating to fashion, music and food and then adopting them as their own. For example, many young British Asians like Bhangra music — a mixture of Punjabi music married with Western rhythms.

Ghuman suggested that Hindu and Sikh girls use compartmentalism to cope with the twin pressures of parental restriction and racial prejudice. He noted that they behave as obedient and respectful daughters, wearing *salwar kameez* and speaking in

Punjabi/Hindi at home, but wearing European-style uniform, speaking English at school and engaging and asserting like their English peers. However, he also noted that some Asian girls have to give up their hope of a career and accept an arranged marriage because of parental pressure. These girls redefine their ethnic identity in terms of conforming to their parents' culture by becoming a 'good' wife and mother.

# Social change and the continuing influence of tradition

While acknowledging the appearance of new ethnic cultural identities, Modood (2001) noted how important traditional values, customs and rituals still are in shaping ethnic identity today. Nearly all Asians, whether they are Pakistani, Bangladeshi or Indian, can understand a community language, and two-thirds use it with other family members younger than themselves.

According to Modood, studies indicate that the overwhelming majority of young British Pakistanis and Bangladeshis return to the collectivistic value system that underpins their upbringing. Most choose to organise their domestic and personal lives on the basis of the values of obligation, duty, community and honour. This behaviour is distinct from their white peers. Studies suggest that this results from two linked realisations, i.e. that the attractions of English lifestyles do not compensate for a lack of family security, and that assimilation into such a culture is pointless because of racism. However, the return to the traditional system involves some modification of their parents' cultural values and norms, especially for females who often now want education and a career.

More than half of married 16–34-year-old British Pakistanis and Bangladeshis have spouses chosen by their parents. Modood concluded that although there has been some decline in belief in traditional values and practices across the younger generation, this does not mean that tradition exercises a weak influence. In fact, in some cultures, especially Muslim ones, tradition is still the main shaper of ethnic identity — Muslim traditional values and practices (i.e. fundamentalism) are experiencing a political and religious revival among Pakistani young men in the early twenty-first century. These young men are demonstrating a profound opposition to Western lifestyles, especially American values, and may express this opposition by resisting white society in a number of ways.

Jacobson (1997) argued that many young Pakistanis are adopting an Islamic identity in terms of diet, dress and everyday routines and practices. She suggests that this is essentially a defensive identity that has developed as a response to racism and social exclusion. Islamic identity compensates for such marginalisation because it stresses the exclusion of the white excluders by those they have excluded.

**Evaluation**

- Ethnic identity is also influenced by social class and race.
- Butler found that young female Muslims were generally happy with the way Islam treated women.
- Generational conflict over arranged marriages is probably exaggerated by the white media.

**Key concepts**

ethnic minority; racism; prejudice; discrimination; institutional racism; generational conflict; dual identity; hybrid cultures

# The role of socialisation in the creation of age identities

The UK segregates its members by age. Consequently, the way in which young and old people are treated has a significant influence on their identity.

## Biology and age

Biology influences the way that society divides people by age. Babies, infants and children are not physically or psychologically developed enough to perform adult tasks, while the ageing process may mean that the elderly are not as physically or as mentally effective as they were when they were younger. However, sociologists point out that there are enough cultural differences across societies and even across sub-cultural groups within the UK to suggest that age differences are also socially or culturally constructed.

## The social and cultural construction of age

In many traditional societies, people often do not know their birth date (meaning they do not celebrate birthdays) or precise age because births are not registered. Generally, people's age identities go through three major stages in traditional societies:

- Children — they are regarded as dependent on older groups for protection and survival.
- Adults — children go through a rite of passage or initiation ceremony, usually at puberty, in which they are instructed in adult ways. Boys may learn how to

be warriors or hunters and have to endure several tests of skill and/or strength. Girls are instructed on sexual matters so that they can become wives and mothers shortly after puberty.

- Elders — as people age in tribal societies, they often acquire greater status and power because they are regarded as having greater experience and wisdom than those who are younger. It is often assumed that a young man should defer without question to his elders.

In contrast, in modern Western societies such as the UK, the state insists that all births are registered. It is taken for granted that people know their birth dates and that they celebrate birthdays.

Bradley (1996) identified five major generational stages of age identity in the UK. Generations are age groups that live through the same historical and social events, and whose common identity and attitudes are reinforced by similar experiences of consuming cultural goods such as fashion, music, films and television programmes. These stages are described in the following sections.

# Childhood

This is regarded as a special, innocent time in which children should be cosseted and protected by their parents. They are supported in this enterprise by the state, which has introduced laws, e.g. various Children's Acts, in order to regulate the quality of parenting. The state has also introduced legislation to create guidelines on what is acceptable behaviour for children, e.g. schooling is compulsory between the ages of 5 and 16, and 10 is the lowest age at which a child can be held responsible for a criminal offence.

Some childhood experts, notably Aries, argue that the experience of childhood identity has changed considerably over the last 500 years. Aries claims that until the nineteenth century, children were generally treated as mini-adults, e.g. they went out to work. Other commentators, such as Postman, argue that the period of childhood has been considerably shortened in the twentieth century, and children today are exposed to too many negative influences, resulting in a loss of innocence.

## Adolescence or youth

This is the period between puberty and the achievement of full adult status, i.e. the teenage years. Until the late 1960s, entrance to adulthood in the UK was usually celebrated on the twenty-first birthday. However, in the last part of the twentieth century, the eighteenth birthday has become a more common milestone, because this is the age at which the state confers legal adulthood via the right to vote, marry or leave home without parental consent and sit on a jury.

In the 1950s, adolescence or youth was recognised as a unique age group for the first time. Before the Second World War, adolescence was generally regarded as part of adulthood, because the majority of youth left school in their early teens and started work. They were not recognised as a separate social category because they were generally indistinguishable from their parents in terms of their values, tastes, behaviour and dress. There was no specific teenage market for fashion, cosmetics and mass media such as films and popular music.

The postwar period saw the emergence of a youth culture based on specific teenage fashions, hairstyles and tastes in music such as rock and roll, which the older generation found shocking and threatening. This culture was the product of an increase in young people's spending power, brought about by full employment in the 1950s. Business reacted to this lucrative new market by developing products specifically for youth, such as comics and magazines for teenagers, pop music, radio stations, transistor radios, fashion and cosmetics.

Studies of the mass media have shown how youth and youth cultures are often demonised by the mass media and subjected to moral panics that create social anxiety about their 'deviance'. Contemporary studies of the mass media's portrayal of teenagers, particularly Thornton (1995) and Savage (2007), suggest that teenagers are condemned more frequently than they are praised by the mass media.

### Evaluation

– Studies of young people suggest that the generation gap implied by moral panics is exaggerated. There is little evidence that youth identity is significantly different in terms of what young people value compared with their parents.
– Most young people are generally conformist — they get on well with their parents and place a high value on traditional goals such as getting married, having children and buying a house.

## Young adulthood

This stage of age identity is focused on the period between leaving the parental home and middle age. Wallace (1992) suggested that modern societies like the UK have private and public 'markers' which signify the beginning of adult status. For example, private markers might include a first sexual encounter or first cigarette, while public markers include the right to vote or the approval of a bank loan. Hockey and James (1993) saw young adulthood as bound up with having freedom and independence from parents, control over material resources and responsibilities.

## Middle age

There is some disagreement as to when middle age begins. Brookes-Gunn and Kirsch (1984) set it as low as 35 years, while others have suggested it might be as high as 50. Physical indicators of middle age include greying hair, the appearance of 'middle-aged spread', the menopause in women. Social indicators include children leaving home for university and more money for leisure pursuits. There may also be emotional or psychological indicators, i.e. the mid-life crisis.

## Old age

This period officially and legally begins at 65 years in the UK, when people are expected to retire from paid work and to draw their state pension. However, Pilcher argues that because of increasing life expectancy and differences in generational attitudes, tastes and behaviour, we should differentiate between the 'young old' (aged 65–74), the 'middle-aged old' (aged 75–84), and the 'old old' (aged 85+).

In contrast to traditional societies, the elderly in the UK are not accorded much respect or status, because work is the major source of status in industrial societies. Loss of work due to retirement can result in a significant decline in self-esteem, social contacts and income, as well as a consequent rise in loneliness, poverty, depression and poor health in general.

# Ageism

The low status associated with elderly identity in UK society is compounded by the fact that people are often stereotyped and discriminated against because of their age. This is known as ageism, and is expressed in three ways:

- It is often institutionalised — it is embedded in organisational and legal practices. Bradley noted that old people may be seen as less suitable for employment because they are assumed to be 'physically slow, lacking in dynamism and not very adaptable to change'.
- It is often expressed through stereotypical prejudices underpinning everyday interaction with elderly people, which assume that a person's competency is limited by their age, i.e. they are too old to carry out a particular task. Pilcher noted that old people are often described in derogatory or condescending ways, especially in mass media representations of youth and old age. Advertising reinforces the view that the appearance of youth is central to looking good and that ageing should be resisted at all costs. Media and popular stereotypes tend to marginalise old people as inferior.
- It assumes that the very old are vulnerable and dependent on younger and fitter adults for care and protection. Ginn and Arber noted that the increasing number of the elderly — in 2002, people aged 60 and over formed for the first time a larger part of the population than children aged under 16 — has led to fears about the costs to society of the elderly, e.g. the rising costs of pensions and of the increased use of health and welfare services. This has resulted in media reports portraying the elderly as a 'burden' on taxpayers.

### Evaluation

It is important to note that the way in which particular age groups or generations are treated is often shaped by influences such as gender, social class and ethnicity. For example, the experience of being an elderly African-Caribbean woman may be different from that of being a white middle-class elderly man.

# Exploring the research process

## What is sociological research?

Sociologists aim to explain the following aspects of the social world or society that we live in:

- why we live in particular social institutions, e.g. the family
- why we allow social institutions to have influence over our lives, e.g. compulsory education, the law, religion
- how our social positions within such societies affect our futures, e.g. social class, gender, ethnicity
- why our society has 'social problems' such as crime, divorce, racism

Sociologists aim to do this by carrying out sociological research. The intention of sociological research is to go beyond 'common sense' and personal experience by collecting evidence or data that give us scientific and objective insight into patterns of behaviour that would otherwise remain hidden. Sociologists use this evidence to construct explanations or theories for why those patterns occur. Research, therefore, leads to sociological theories of human behaviour.

## The purpose of sociological research

### Gathering data about the social world

The first task of research is to gather information or data about the society in which we live.

Sociologists use two broad types of data:

- Primary data are gathered 'first-hand' by the sociologist using a variety of methods, for example, by asking people questions via questionnaires or interviews or by observing their behaviour.
- Secondary data are collected by people who are not sociologists, and published or written down. For example, crime statistics are collected by the police and the courts and are collated and published by civil servants at the Home Office every 3 months. Journalists may research crime and publish their findings in the form of newspaper or magazine articles.

The form taken by data can differ. Some data appear in the form of numbers or statistics, and are called quantitative data. They can be displayed in tables, graphs, bar charts, pie charts, tally charts, columns of figures and lists of percentages. This type of data tends to be very factual.

Other data take a written form and provide a more personal account of the social world, e.g. they might be in the form of transcripts or summaries of interviews, selected quotations from conversations, descriptions of a place, a group or a situation, or in the form of a diary entry. This type of data is known as qualitative data, and tends to be concerned with how people see or interpret the world around them, often giving a first-hand account or insight into the feelings, opinions, motivations and thoughts of those being researched. Qualitative evidence allows those being studied to speak for themselves.

## Making correlations

Research can go further than gathering information, and can help us explore relationships between different elements of society. This can be in the form of simple correlations (showing that two things are linked in some way). For example, there is a statistical relationship between drug use and crime — when heroin addiction levels are high, property crimes such as burglary tend to rise.

## Developing theories

Research can support or disprove a sociological theory (an explanation of social events). Researchers gather information and statistics that help sociologists to explain why certain social events occur, which often involves providing an explanation with correlations. For example, if a correlation exists between drug use and crime, various theories can be developed, e.g. that heroin users are more likely to commit burglary because they need money to pay for their drug habit. An alternative theory is that burglars have a high income and are more likely to have a pleasurable lifestyle that involves using drugs.

# Research methods available to sociologists

The most common methods of sociological data collection are:
- The survey questionnaire — these are lists of questions that are normally distributed to large groups of people, either by hand or by post. The respondent writes the answers him/herself, in a process known as self-completion.
- Interviews — these are questions asked by trained interviewers, to which answers are given verbally. There are two broad types of interview. First, the structured interview, in which an interviewer asks questions using a pre-determined questionnaire (called an 'interview schedule'). Second, the unstructured interview, which is more like a conversation — the interviewer's questions often depend on the answers given by the interviewee.

- Observation — people's behaviour is watched by sociologists. For example, the sociologist may sit in a classroom and observe the interaction between a teacher and the class, counting the number of contributions made by male and female students or the number of times a student is praised or disciplined. In some observations, the sociologist joins in with the everyday life of those he/she is watching. For example, he/she might watch how people on a train respond to somebody using a mobile phone loudly.
- The analysis of secondary data — this involves examining existing material such as official statistics, historical documents or diaries. For example, in order to understand which social groups are more likely to commit crime, sociologists look at the criminal statistics because these give an insight into the social backgrounds of offenders.

Central to success in this unit is knowledge and understanding of four key concepts — reliability, validity, representativeness and generalisability — and the ways in which they might affect the design of a piece of research and its findings. These concepts are the tools which you should use to evaluate the effectiveness of research.

## Reliability

Reliability is a concept usually applied to the way the data are collected, i.e. the research method or measurement procedure. It generally refers to whether the same or similar results would be produced if the research were repeated by the same researcher or by other sociologists.

Reliability is important to sociologists who want to carry out research that is as scientific as possible and who wish to generate quantitative data. These sociologists are called positivists.

Survey questionnaires and structured interviews are generally regarded as the most reliable and scientific primary research methods available to sociologists. With regards to secondary data, official statistics, e.g. birth, death and crime statistics, are also seen as highly reliable because they are usually collected in a standardised way.

### Evaluation

- When research is repeated, results may differ if the circumstances or environment have changed, e.g. a repeat interview may be contaminated by the experience of the earlier interview.
- Reliable methods can produce invalid results, e.g. the British Crime Survey is a victim survey based on a highly standardised questionnaire, but people may not respond honestly to its questions if they feel humiliated by being a victim of crime.

## Validity

Validity is a concept that generally refers to whether research and its findings give a true picture of what is being studied, i.e. whether it reflects the reality of the activities or attitudes of the person/group being studied.

Validity is important to researchers who want to establish the meanings that people attach to their actions. These sociologists are called interpretivists. They are interested in how the group being studied thinks and feels. They usually collect qualitative, rather than quantitative, data.

The primary methods of data collection commonly used by such sociologists are participant observation, non-participant observation and unstructured interviews. Interpretivist sociologists also see the secondary data obtained from expressive documents such as diaries and letters as high in validity.

**Evaluation**

- The results of research may be a product of the research method rather than the reality of what is being studied.
- People may sometimes tell the researcher what they think he/she would like to hear — this type of interview bias reduces validity.
- The social characteristics of the researcher may influence what the people/group being studied say — this type of interview bias reduces validity.
- People in a group may change their behaviour if they think they are being watched — this is known as the Hawthorne effect.
- The researcher may interpret what he/she sees in a different way from that intended by the individuals or group being studied — researcher bias may reduce validity.

## Representativeness

This concept generally means that the group being studied is typical of the population that the researcher is interested in. The sampling unit — the individual or group being researched — should resemble the characteristics of the research population as a whole in terms of social class, age, gender, ethnicity etc. The sample must therefore be a good cross-section of the group.

The researcher must avoid bias when selecting a sample, or validity will be undermined, e.g. the results of a survey into the extent and character of religious belief may be invalid if only those who attend Christian churches regularly are included in the sample.

**Evaluation**

+ Random sampling techniques are generally better suited to gathering representative samples.
- Non-random techniques such as opportunity sampling, i.e. selecting individuals or groups who happen to be available, generally do not produce representative samples.

## Generalisability

Sociologists use representative samples because they want to make claims about the behaviour and attitudes of a larger group, of which the sample is a typical cross-section. They want to say that because the sample behaves or thinks in a particular way, it is highly likely that people similar to those included in the sample will also behave/think in this way.

### Evaluation

– People may share the same social characteristics but interpret the same social situations in different ways.

### Key concepts

reliability; replication; quantitative methods of data collection; positivism; validity; primary methods; secondary data; survey population; representativeness; generalisability; typicality; qualitative methods of data collection; observation; unstructured interviews; interpretivist sociology; interview bias; researcher bias; Hawthorne effect

# Ethical issues

Ethical issues are also important, because research can have a powerful impact on people's lives. The researcher must always think carefully about the impact of the research and how he/she ought to behave, so that no harm comes to the research subject or to society in general. Ethics or moral principles must guide research. There is a growing awareness that research subjects have rights and that researchers have responsibilities and obligations towards them. Generally, British sociologists agree that six broad ethical rules should underpin all sociological research:

- Informed consent — many researchers believe that all research participants have a right to know what the research is about and to refuse to take part or to answer particular questions. People should know research is being carried out on them and how the results will be used so that they can make an intelligent choice as to whether they should take part. However, informed consent is not always a straightforward matter. For example, very young children or people with learning disabilities may not be able to understand fully what the researcher is doing.
- Deception — this occurs when information is kept from research participants or when researchers lie to their subjects about the purpose of the research. Subjects may even be unaware that they are participating in a research study. Deception therefore must be avoided at all costs.
- Privacy — most sociologists agree that the privacy of research subjects should be safeguarded as much as possible. However, sociological research is by its nature intrusive — sociologists are generally interested in what goes on in families, how people behave, what they think etc.
- Confidentiality — the problem of maintaining privacy can be countered by keeping the identity of research participants secret. Confidentiality means that the information an individual gives to the researcher cannot be traced back to that individual. Ethical researchers are careful to disguise the identity of individual participants when they write up their research. If participants know that they

cannot be identified, they may be more willing to reveal personal and private matters to the researcher. In other words, confidentiality may increase the validity of the data collected.

- Protection from harm — most sociologists agree that research participants should be protected from any sort of physical harm, and this is seldom a problem. One of the reasons that sociologists rarely use experiments, for example, is that these may lead to the subjects being harmed. However, some sociological research may harm participants emotionally, for example by asking insensitive questions. Victims of crime may be upset by the information that researchers obtain about the perpetrators, as they may prefer to forget the incident. Sociological research may also have harmful social consequences. For example, people's reputations may be damaged or they may be exposed to ridicule. Participants may face punishment because of something a sociologist published.
- Legality and immorality — sociologists should avoid being drawn into situations where they may commit crimes or assist/witness deviant acts. Sociologists have not always avoided this type of behaviour, especially in terms of the method of observation used (see page 58).

All the above ethical problems are important, because if people do not trust sociologists, then the validity of the data collected by the sociologists will not reflect what respondents are truly thinking or doing.

### Evaluation

- Abiding by the law may risk the researcher's access to a criminal or deviant group or undermine the participant's trust in the researcher. Dick Hobbs and Howard Parker engaged in illegal activities in order to maintain the trust of petty criminals and juvenile delinquents respectively.
- Being honest may lead to the Hawthorne effect, i.e. the people being researched may act in artificial ways if they know a researcher is present.

### Key concepts

privacy; confidentiality; informed consent; illegal activities; Hawthorne effect

# Theoretical constraints on choice of research method

Textbooks often state that whether a sociologist is positivist or interpretivist will affect how research is carried out, and these two ways of viewing the world have dominated sociology for many years. At AS, you must have an awareness of these two traditions and how they may affect the collection of data. At A2, you should know them in detail and be able to mount a theoretical critique.

# How positivism views the social world

Positivists believe that society (the social world) can be studied in an objective way. They note that social patterns and trends exist that suggest human or social behaviour is the product of external social forces — human behaviour is the product of the ways in which societies are organised or structured. Such behaviour is predictable.

Positivists believe that society and the social forces that underpin it can be studied in a logical, systematic way using scientific methods, i.e. those that are regarded as objective (free from the values of the researcher) and high in reliability. These methods include survey questionnaires, structured interviews, experiments and the analysis of official statistics. They aim to collect quantitative data in order to establish cause-and-effect relationships between social phenomena, such as social behaviour, and aspects of social structure, such as social class.

### Evaluation

- Humans have free will and cannot be studied scientifically.
- Links between two variables do not necessarily mean they are related in terms of cause and effect. For example, women are now in a position to pursue a career and divorce has become easier to obtain but, while these two facts may be linked, it is not possible to argue that one has caused the other.
- Quantitative data may tell us more about the groups involved in their collection than the social phenomena they are meant to describe.
- Quantitative data are seen to be high in reliability, but they can be low in validity. For example, crime statistics can be collected repeatedly but they tell us about crimes reported rather than the reality of the amount and extent of crime in society.

### Key concepts

positivism; quantitative methods of data collection; cause and effect; social laws; social structure; reliability; validity

# How interpretivism views the social world

Interpretivists believe that human behaviour is not determined by social laws and is consequently not predictable, because humans can exercise choice and make decisions to pursue alternative courses of action. Individuals are therefore active rather than passive. They create their own destinies rather than having them shaped by social structures.

Interpretivists consider the social world to be socially constructed — it is the product of shared interaction and the meanings or interpretations that humans use to make sense of that interaction. The role of sociologists is to uncover these shared interpretations.

Interpretivists argue that the aim of sociological research should be to get inside people's heads and experience the world from their point of view. This is called empathetic understanding, or *verstehen*. They therefore emphasise the use of ethnographic methods such as unstructured interviews and participant observation, which aims to conduct research in the natural environment of the research subjects and to see the world from their perspective. These methods stress that the validity of the research data is more important than reliability.

**Evaluation**

— Qualitative evidence may be the product of the interpretations of researchers, because they select the data they feel are important, which may reflect their prejudices.

## Combining theoretical perspectives

Many sociologists today combine theoretical perspectives — they believe social behaviour to be the result of a combination of choice and structural influences. For example, educational success may be held back by factors beyond our control, such as our social class, gender and/or ethnicity, but some working-class children defy the odds and succeed or redefine success to fit their own experience.

Consequently, sociologists today tend to use whatever method is most suitable for the situation. A variety of methods (see triangulation on page 63) are usually adopted in order to generate quantitative data supported by qualitative information. For example, questionnaire survey data may be backed up by data from unstructured interviews or observation.

**Key concepts**

validity; subjectivity; *verstehen*; interpretations; meanings; social construction; empathetic understanding; interaction; agency; ethnographic; qualitative data; conversational analysis

# Starting points for sociological research

## The hypothesis

Once a topic or issue has been identified as worthy of study, the researcher needs a starting point for his/her research. The first stage in any research project is to read what others have published on the subject he/she is interested in researching in order to avoid repeating what somebody else has already done. Such reading will provide the researcher with initial data and ideas about how to approach the topic or issue.

Reading will also provide the researcher with ideas for the aims of his/her own research or for a hypothesis that he/she wishes to test. An hypothesis is a 'hunch', usually in the form of a statement that the researcher believes might be true and which can be tested. It is a prediction of what the research will find.

For example: 'Students who study AS sociology watch the televised news more often than students who do not study AS sociology' is an hypothesis. It can be tested by collecting evidence about the televised news-watching habits of the two categories of student. This will confirm or reject the hypothesis, or suggest what further research is needed.

In some studies, theories are 'grounded' in the data collected — the researcher does not have a clear hypothesis, but starts with a general aim and develops the hypothesis and theories as the data collection proceeds.

## Operationalising the hypothesis

Once the researcher has decided on the hypothesis or research question, he/she must think about how to break it down into something that can be observed or measured. Any concepts in the hypothesis or research question must also be broken down. This process is known as 'operationalisation'. For example, the hypothesis, 'Working-class children are more likely to truant from school and commit acts of delinquency', gives rise to five questions of operationalisation:

- What is meant by 'working class'? Social class is not an easy concept to operationalise because it may not mean the same thing to everyone. There are also practical problems to overcome when using this concept, e.g. is the social class of a child that of its father (by job?), mother, or both?
- What is meant by 'children'? Does the researcher intend to include all children of school age, i.e. 4–16, or will he/she focus purely on secondary schoolchildren? If the researcher chooses the latter, does he/she intend to break them down by age group, subject, ability sets etc?
- What is meant by 'more likely'? This implies that the researcher intends to compare working-class children with another group, presumably middle-class children. How will he/she identify the latter? What will be the main point of comparison?
- What is meant by 'truancy'? Is the researcher using an official definition of truancy, and is this shared by the headteacher, the teachers and the students of the school being used? Will it mean complete days off without parents' permission or knowledge? What about students who miss certain lessons when in school or students who register and then truant?
- What is meant by 'delinquency'? This is a wide-ranging concept. What activities would be included in the research? How will the researcher make sure that his/her definition is shared by the people taking part in the research?

## Operationalising the concepts of social class and ethnicity

Social class is a difficult term to define and operationalise, and is usually based on the jobs we do. Manual workers — people who generally use their hands or strength in their jobs — are seen as working class, but can be further divided into categories based on skills levels. Workers who possess a scarce skill that is the product of an apprenticeship or vocational qualification, e.g. electricians or plumbers, or who occupy a supervisory position, e.g. foremen, generally have a higher class position than manual workers who are semi-skilled or unskilled.

Non-manual workers are generally regarded as middle class, and again can be divided into categories. Executives responsible for the day-to-day operational control of companies are generally regarded as having more status than lower professionals such as teachers and white-collar workers.

Occupation is therefore regarded by many sociologists as a good indicator of social class. It also generally indicates other status factors, such as level of education (e.g. most professionals went to university, whereas many non-skilled labourers did not) and whether people own their home (e.g. middle-class people are more likely to be owner-occupiers, whereas most council tenants come from working-class backgrounds). Some sociologists have even suggested that social class can be determined using postal codes.

In the past, the government used a system called the Registrar General's Scale of Social Class, which ranked jobs into five social classes according to skill and education. People in the UK were ranked as either middle class (class I — professional and higher managerial, class II — lower professional and managerial or class IIIN — skilled, non-manual, e.g. white-collar worker) or working-class (IIIM — skilled manual, e.g. plumber, IV — partly skilled, e.g. bus-driver or V — unskilled, e.g. building labourer).

In 2000, this system was abandoned. Sociologists had been critical of it for some time because it did not include people who did not work or who lived off their wealth, it was based purely on male occupation — women were classified on the basis of the job of either their husband or father — and it contained many contradictions, e.g. lower professionals in social class II were often paid less than skilled manual workers in social class IIIM.

A new system of officially categorising social class was put in place in 2000. The National Statistics Socio-Economic Classification (NS-SEC) is based on 'employment relations and conditions'. People are still classed according to their occupation but jobs are now ranked into eight social classes based on job security, opportunities for promotion and the ability of the worker to make decisions on his/her own.

Ethnicity can also be a difficult concept to categorise. Many people think that it refers to 'race' or skin colour. However, it actually refers to shared cultural characteristics which may include language, religion, history, traditions, family and marriage patterns and a sense of shared identity. Determining someone's ethnicity can be complicated. For example, 'white' has frequently been used by researchers as a category, but do white English, Welsh, Scots and Irish people share the same perspective? The answer is no, and differences in ethnicity therefore exist between them.

The modern UK is a multicultural society. Sociologists used 'black' as a category in the past, which is now seen as a redundant concept, for a number of reasons. For example, intermarriage between African-Caribbeans and whites has resulted in more mixed-race (sometimes called 'dual-heritage') couples and children now than ever before. The term 'Asian' is also no longer useful, because of the national and religious differences within this group.

Operationalisation of concepts is an important part of the research process. Precise measurement of social phenomena cannot occur without it.

## Operationalising the research population

The research population is the group being studied by the sociologist. It is important to be precise about its definition, e.g. 'children', 'young people' and 'teenagers' are vague groups. In order to study any of these groups, the sociologist would need to identify their precise age range. Moreover, the sociologist would need to make a decision about whether the research was aimed at individuals, households, families, schools etc. For example, if the researcher was looking at teenagers in education, what types of school or college would he or she attempt to access?

## Access issues

Sociological researchers need to think carefully about how they are going to access the institution in which their research group is most likely to be found. For example, if the research is focused on young teenagers, this group is most likely to be found in a school. Researchers would gain access to this group by writing to local education authorities and head teachers for permission to enter schools. If the research was to focus on teenagers under the age of 16, parental informed consent would need to be sought. Sociological researchers would also have to make decisions about the number and type of schools that would take part in the study. Sociologists might wish to carry out comparative research by comparing a school in a middle-class suburb with one in a deprived area which has a disproportionate number of working-class and ethnic minority students, or by comparing schools in different parts of the country (this raises issues of which towns and cities are typical of each region).

Researchers might also wish to focus on the elderly, but this is a difficult group to access. It is a broad group, and sociologists often resort to distinguishing between the 'young old' (aged 60–75) and the 'elderly old' (aged 75+). Residential homes are unlikely to provide representative samples of the elderly because they contain disproportionate numbers of the 'elderly old' and the senile. Accessing sheltered housing is also unlikely to result in a representative sample, because most elderly people still live in their own homes. Some sociologists have accessed sea-side retirement towns like Bridlington or Bournemouth, and approached elderly people in the street or in places that they are likely to frequent, e.g. libraries, post offices on pension days.

Some sociologists have accessed particular groups via the internet, e.g. through chat rooms or interactive sites such as MySpace or Bebo. Some researchers have even set up interactive research sites where they post notices asking for volunteers, or questionnaires for internet users to complete.

content guidance

# Sampling techniques

It is usually too expensive and time-consuming to ask everybody in a research population to take part in research. Most researchers select a sample that is representative (i.e. a typical cross-section) of the population they are interested in. With a representative sample, it is possible to generalise to the wider research population — what is true of the sample should be true of the research population as a whole.

Two main sampling techniques can be used to ensure that the sample is representative of the wider research population: random sampling and non-random sampling.

### Random sampling

A simple random sample involves selecting names randomly from a list or sampling frame. Using this technique, every member of the research population has an equal chance of being included in the sample, so those chosen are likely to be a cross-section of the population.

Types of sampling frames include:
- the electoral register (a list of people aged over 18 years who are registered to vote)
- the Postcode Address File
- the telephone directory
- school attendance registers
- GP's patient records

All sampling frames are unsatisfactory in some respect — not everyone is included, they are often out of date and some groups may be over-represented while other groups may not be included. A simple random sample therefore does not guarantee a representative sample — a researcher may select too many young people, too many males etc. Sociologists have developed three variations on the random sample in order to produce representative samples:
- Systematic sampling involves randomly choosing a number between 1 and 10, e.g. 7, and then identifying every tenth number from that point, e.g. 7, 17, 27, 37, from the sampling frame until the sample is complete. This does not always guarantee a representative sample, but the larger the sample, the more likely it is to be representative.
- Stratified sampling is the most common form of random sampling used in sociological research. It involves dividing the research population into a number of sampling frames. For example, if researchers were sampling students at a college, and discovered that 60% of students were female and 40% were male, they would want their sample to reflect those proportions. The sampling frame, i.e. college registers, would need to be transformed into two sampling frames, i.e. a list of female students and a list of male students. If the researchers intended to have an overall sample of 100 students, they would then randomly select 60 female and 40 male students from their two lists. Researchers could, if necessary, construct sampling frames based on age, ethnicity, qualifications or courses.

- Cluster sampling uses a map, often in cases where there is no specific list of people available. The researcher may randomly select two districts, and then randomly select streets within those districts. The researcher then targets a further sample of people or households within the streets. This technique is attractive to some researchers because areas are often characterised by social class or ethnic clusters, and so offer easy access to particular social groups, e.g. working-class and ethnic minority communities.

### Non-random sampling

- Quota sampling is often used by market research companies to target people in the street to talk about consumer products. The researcher is told by his/her company how many participants are needed in each category, and goes looking for them. For example, if a researcher needs to interview 50 women aged 40–55 who live in north Yorkshire, he or she goes to where such people are likely to be found, e.g. a town centre in north Yorkshire, and asks people whether they are willing to be interviewed, until the quota is filled. This sampling technique is often used by the media to find out people's voting preferences before an election.
- Purposive or opportunity sampling involves researchers choosing individuals or cases that fit the nature of the research. For example, a researcher interested in how skateboarders in Leeds see themselves might access a local skateboarding park at a weekend and ask all those present to take part in the research.
- Snowball sampling is used mainly when it is difficult to gain access to a particular group of people because there is no sampling frame available or because they engage in deviant or illegal activities that are normally carried out in isolation or in secret. This technique involves finding and interviewing a person who fits the research needs and then asking him/her to suggest another person who might be willing to be interviewed. The sample can grow as large as the researcher wants. Plant (1975) used this type of sampling technique in his study of cannabis use. However, snowball sampling may not produce a representative sample.

All sampling is a compromise between representativeness and practicality, and researchers often have to make do with samples that are not fully representative. The most important requirement of any research when it comes to sampling is to be aware of any potential bias caused by the sampling technique, and to report fully on this in the analysis of the research findings.

### Evaluation

- Care must be taken when using electoral rolls or registers (lists of households) because they may be incomplete — some people avoid paying council tax, people die or move away, the homeless are excluded and children below the age of 18 are not included.
- A telephone directory excludes those who do not have telephones or who have ex-directory numbers. Therefore, a sociological investigation into people's perceptions of privacy might run into problems if a telephone directory is used as the sampling frame.

- Sometimes sampling frames are inaccessible because of ethical issues such as privacy and confidentiality. For example, a doctor is unlikely to agree to allow researchers to access his/her patients' files.
- Sampling frames are not objective or neutral sources of information — they reflect the interests and prejudices of the people who compile them. For example, school registers from a comprehensive school in an affluent suburb are likely to contain an over-proportionate number of middle-class white pupils.
- There are unlikely to be sampling frames of deviant or criminal groups available.

**Key concepts**

survey population; sample; sampling frame; random sampling; non-random sampling; representativeness; generalisations; typicality; probability

# Operationalisation of the hypothesis/research question

Once a sociologist decides on a research question/hypothesis, it must be developed and broken down into a set of components or indicators that can be observed and measured. For example, if 'fear of crime' is the central research focus, the researcher needs to define the term precisely, in a way that is shared by a potential survey population. Once the definition is agreed on, the researcher must identify components of 'fear of crime' that can be turned into questions suitable for a questionnaire/interview schedule, or categories of behaviour that can be recorded on an observation schedule.

It is important that questions or categories used in observation/content analysis schedules do not reflect the researcher's own values, interpretations and prejudices. It is also important that questions and categories do not 'force' respondents into making artificial responses. Loaded (emotional, subjective) questions, e.g. 'Are you a racist?', and leading questions, e.g. 'Don't you think sex before marriage is disgusting?', should be avoided.

**Evaluation**

- Interpretivists argue that a value-free type of research is impossible — sociologists always impose their view of reality on respondents through questions etc.
- They also argue that research methods like questionnaires and structured interviews are artificial — people do not normally experience them on an everyday basis and are therefore likely to react in artificial ways.
- Operationalisation is regarded as unreliable by interpretivists because different sociologists may operationalise and measure hypotheses and research questions differently.

**Key concepts**

operationalisation; hypothesis

# Research methods

## Social or sample surveys

Social or sample surveys are methods of research often used by positivists, which enable the researcher to gain large quantities of data from a representative sample of the survey population. The research device/tool is often a questionnaire, although structured interviews can also be used.

Surveys can be snapshot (a group is studied at a particular period in time) or longitudinal (a group is studied over a period of years). Parker's research on drug use took 5 years, while Douglas's study of child-rearing and parental interest in education took place over two decades.

### Questionnaires

A questionnaire is a list of questions written down in advance, and is the main method for gathering data in social surveys. It may be administered in a number of ways, such as by post, through magazines and newspapers, by hand, via the internet or e-mail. Respondents complete questionnaires for themselves (if a questionnaire is completed on behalf of a respondent by a researcher, it is an interview schedule).

When constructing a questionnaire, the sociologist has to ensure the following:
- It must ask the right questions, which unearth exactly the information wanted — the questions must be focused, i.e. they should operationalise the key components of the research question or hypothesis.
- The questions should be asked in a clear and simple manner that can be understood by the respondents. Therefore, the researcher must think carefully about the language used in the question. Ideally, questions should be neutral and objective — they must not 'lead' respondents into the answers required by the researcher, and they should not be 'loaded', i.e. written in such a way that respondents are provoked into emotional responses that evade the truth. They should also avoid technical and vague vocabulary. It is important to ensure that all respondents share the same understanding of the questions.
- The questionnaire should be as short as possible, because people are usually unwilling to spend a long time completing questionnaires.

**Questionnaire design**

Questionnaires use a variety of question types. The most common are closed questions and open questions.

Closed questionnaires usually have a series of questions with a choice of answers — the respondent has to tick the box next to the most appropriate answer. Such questionnaires are quantitative — they produce lots of statistical data.

Open questionnaires ask open-ended questions — the respondent is asked to write down what he/she feels or has experienced. Such questionnaires are qualitative, i.e. the data are concerned with how respondents see the world.

In addition, a self report is a type of questionnaire that, when used in the sociological study of crime and deviance, lists a number of criminal activities and asks respondents to tick those they have committed. Anonymity and confidentiality are usually guaranteed.

Attitude questionnaires usually ask respondents whether they subscribe to a particular point of view, using a scale of 1–5 where 1 represents 'strongly agree', 3 represents 'neutral' and 5 represents 'strongly disagree'.

## Strengths of questionnaires
- They can be used for reaching a large number of people, since the questionnaire can be handed out.
- Postal questionnaires can be used if the research population is widely dispersed or if information is required from different areas.
- They are less time-consuming than other methods, such as interviewing.
- They are reasonably cheap to carry out compared with other methods, e.g. interviewing might require the recruitment of an interviewing team.
- They are useful for research that intends to ask embarrassing or sensitive questions about sexual activities or illegal acts. People may be more likely to tell the truth if the questionnaires guarantee anonymity than if they have to face an interviewer.
- They can produce lots of statistical data, which can be compared and correlated.
- The sociologist has minimum contact with the respondent in self-completion and therefore should not influence the results.
- They are thought to be high in reliability. Another researcher using the same questionnaire should achieve similar results if the questions are neutral and objective.
- They are thought to be high in validity because if everyone is answering exactly the same questions, they are responding to the same thing. Any difference in the answers should reflect differences in real life.

## Weaknesses of questionnaires
- Many people do not make the effort to reply to questionnaires, especially postal ones — they suffer from non-response. The number of questionnaires returned can be very low, e.g. the Hite Report on attitudes towards sex in the USA was based on the return of 3,000 questionnaires from the 100,000 sent out. The returned questionnaires may therefore not be representative of the research population — those who have replied may have strong views, whereas the rest of the population may have moderate views.
- It is difficult to go into any depth in a questionnaire because the questions need to be as clear and simple as possible.

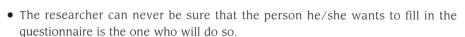

- The researcher can never be sure that the person he/she wants to fill in the questionnaire is the one who will do so.
- Respondents may interpret the question in a different way from that intended by the researcher, and their responses may mean something different from what the researcher believes they mean. This undermines validity.
- Validity is not guaranteed, because respondents may deceive the researcher for a variety of reasons. They may not tell the truth because they feel threatened, e.g. because they believe that the researcher will socially disapprove of certain types of behaviour or because the researcher is prying into an aspect of their lives that they regard as sensitive and/or private. They may even exaggerate their response, e.g. young males may lie because they feel the truth undermines their masculinity.
- Critics suggest that questionnaires result in the imposition of the sociologist's view of the world — the questions asked are the those that the sociologist, rather than the respondent, has decided are important.
- Respondents are often unable to elaborate on their feelings and emotions in a questionnaire because the design does not allow detail or depth in responses.
- People like to manage the impression that others have of them, and this can shape their responses to a questionnaire. For example, people often answer in the affirmative to questions asking if they attend church (despite not doing so) to give an impression of themselves as upright, decent and respectable citizens.

### Pilot studies or surveys

Pilot studies or surveys are carried out prior to a main study in order to check the effectiveness of the questionnaire and the sampling technique. Although pilot studies can be used with any method of data collection, they are most commonly used with social surveys.

Piloting, or trialling, can save time and money if there is a problem with the research device (questionnaire, interview schedule etc.). The following aspects can be checked:
- the questions, e.g. those that do not work or that are unclear can be reworded
- the ease of access to the sample
- the appropriateness of the sample
- the sampling technique, e.g. the response rate can be estimated

## Interviews

Interviews of all types are generally recorded manually (i.e. written down) and/or recorded/videoed in order to produce a transcript from which quotations illustrating the point of view of the respondent can be used to support (or contradict) a particular hypothesis.

Interviews can be carried out in a public space, e.g. on the street by market researchers, on the telephone or on the internet in chatrooms. However, most successful interviews are carried out privately in neutral and unthreatening venues.

The advantage of all types of interview is their adaptability. A skilful interviewer can follow up ideas, probe responses and investigate motives and feelings, which the questionnaire can never do. The way in which a response is made (the tone of voice, facial expression, hesitation etc.) can provide information that a written response might conceal. Questionnaire responses have to be taken at face value, but a response in an interview can be developed and clarified.

Interviews are particularly useful when studying areas which are not accessible to study using other methods. For example, it would be impractical to observe house-work or childcare, and somebody who is regarded as 'deviant' may not respond to a questionnaire.

## Structured interviews

A structured interview involves the researcher reading out a list of questions and writing down the respondent's answers. Such interviews allow little flexibility, i.e. the interviewer is not normally allowed to deviate from the questions on the interview schedule. Responses to these types of interviews are usually expressed in quantita-tive form.

### Strengths of structured interviews

- The interviewer can add to the survey data by observing the social context of responses, e.g. the facial expression, tone of voice, body language and attitude of the respondent. The interviewer can record information about the respondent, where he/she lives, his/her social status etc., that could prove useful in inter-preting the respondent's motives or any vague answers that he/she may have given.
- The focus on closed questions and fixed categories means that they are useful for collecting factual data in a statistical or quantitative form, which can be presented easily in a table or graph.
- Samples can be reasonably large if each interview is conducted quickly, i.e. between 10 and 30 minutes.
- They can ensure that the right person responds to the questions, unlike postal questionnaires (PQs).
- An interviewer can ask for clarification of vague answers, although he/she must usually stick to the script rather than veering off in interesting directions.
- An interviewer can explain the aims and objectives of the research, clarify instruc-tions and make sure the respondent is happy with the research. This reduces potential non-response.
- Interviews have better response rates than PQs, because the interviewer can return if a potential respondent is not at home.

### Weaknesses of structured interviews

- The structured interview experiences the same problems as the questionnaire. Interviews are artificial devices which are not a normal part of everyday reality — people may therefore respond to them with suspicion, i.e. they may feel that any information they give the interviewer may be used against them, so they may fail to complete the interview.
- Respondents' answers may contain evasive, partial or false information.

- Interviews that use closed questions with category/list responses suffer from the 'imposition problem'— they measure what the sociologist thinks is important rather than what the interviewee experiences. By choosing particular questions and responses, the interviewer has already mapped out the experiences, interpretations etc. of the respondents and consequently may fail to ask the really important questions.
- Interviewees may be forced to tick boxes that only approximate to their experiences and views, which will undermine the validity of the data. Other respondents become frustrated that their experiences or views are not reflected in the questions or category/list responses and fail to complete the interview.
- Interviewing is unsuitable for studies that require very large samples — especially those that are dispersed across the country. Interview samples are therefore less likely to be representative than questionnaire survey samples.
- Structured interviews, like questionnaires, often depend on memory — respondents may exaggerate, underestimate or telescope specific events in their lives and therefore give the interviewer invalid data.
- There is often a gap between what people say they do and what they actually do — people do not like to put their prejudices into action, or they are not aware that they behave in certain ways.

## Unstructured interviews

An unstructured interview is like a guided conversation, where the talk is informal but the researcher asks questions to ensure that the participant keeps to the subject of the research. The interviewer does not usually have an interview schedule — unstructured interviews are flexible, because although the interviewer has an idea of the topics to cover, he or she can follow the respondent if this might produce useful results, and has freedom to allow the interview to follow its own course. Unstructured interviews are usually conducted in a place convenient to the interviewee, such as at home, in a local café or in a park, so that the interviewee feels as relaxed and comfortable as possible.

### Strengths of unstructured interviews

- They allow the researcher to establish a relationship with the respondent, i.e. trust and rapport. This encourages more valid qualitative responses, which can then be analysed.
- They are particularly suited to researching sensitive groups, i.e. people who might be suspicious of or hostile to outsiders. They allow the interviewer to explain the purpose of the research, and normally stress the anonymity and confidentiality of the research report.
- Their organisation focuses on what the interviewee says or thinks — the respondent is placed at the centre of the research. Respondents may be more likely to discuss sensitive and painful experiences if they feel that the interviewer is sympathetic, understanding and truly interested.
- They offer respondents greater opportunity to take control, define priorities and direct the interview into areas they think are important. This can lead to new and

important insights for the researcher. If respondents feel at ease, they are more likely to open up and say what they really feel and mean.

- They allow the interviewer to make sure that he/she ascribes the same meaning to an issue as the interviewee.
- They provide richer, more vivid and more colourful data than questionnaires or structured interviews, although such data are often time-consuming to transcribe and can be difficult to analyse and compare because of the volume of material in the respondent's own words.

### Weaknesses of unstructured interviews

Some sociologists criticise unstructured interviews for being unscientific — they lack a number of characteristics seen as essential in scientific research:

- They are seen to be lacking in reliability — every interview is different because it depends on the unique relationship established between the interviewer and interviewee. Therefore, they cannot be replicated and checked.
- They are thought to be lacking in objectivity, because the researcher has a personal relationship with the interviewee. Moreover, the data are not gathered objectively — the interviewer often selects aspects of the interview transcripts that fit the hypothesis. This may reflect the ideological biases of the researcher, e.g. what is left out of the final analysis may contradict the hypothesis. For example, Paul Willis used quotations from his interviews with working-class lads to illustrate how they opposed the school system, but he may have selectively ignored material from his interview transcripts which showed the lads conforming.
- Unstructured interviews are exceptionally time-consuming to conduct and transcribe. Consequently, sociological research which uses unstructured interviews tends to use fewer participants than surveys do. Positivists claim that interview participants tend to be less representative of the research population as a result.
- Because of the nature of unstructured interviews and the data that they generate, it is difficult to construct a comparative analysis of data from different interviews and therefore to generalise from them to similar populations in the wider community.

### Semi-structured interviews

Many sociological interviews are a mix of the structured and unstructured — each interview usually has the same set of questions, but the interviewer is given the freedom and flexibility to 'probe'. Semi-structured interviews, therefore, allow the interviewer to ask respondents for clarification of vague answers and to follow up and develop their responses. For example, the interviewer can jog respondents' memories and ask them to give examples. These, and other techniques, can add depth and detail to responses, and can assess the truthfulness of the participant. However, the reliability of such interviews has been questioned, because an interviewer might find that some interviewees need more probing than others. This may mean that every interview is different, so the data may not be strictly comparable — to some extent, the interviewees are responding to different questions.

## Focus-group and group interviews

Some interviews are carried out with groups rather than individuals — the interviewer talks to a panel of respondents (usually between 8 and 10 people). Group interviews usually involve people getting together to discuss an issue, rather than simply giving an answer to a question. They are normally used when the researcher wants to explore the dynamics of a group, because he/she believes that a truer picture emerges when the group is together. Mac an Ghaill (1994) used this method when he gathered a group of gay students to discuss their experience of school.

A variation on the group/panel interview is the focus-group interview, in which participants are encouraged to talk to each other. This method was first used by market researchers to see how consumers responded to particular products, and has since been adopted by political parties and sociologists. An interviewer guides the participants — who may be asked to discuss particular questions or topics — but relies on the dynamics of the group to keep it going, i.e. there is minimal interference. The interaction is usually recorded on audiotape or video. One danger of group interviews is that participants with strong personalities can dominate and influence other participants' opinions.

## General problems with interviewing

The biggest methodological concern with interviewing in all its forms is interviewer bias — which occurs when the interviewer influences the responses given by the interviewee. Such bias is often unavoidable, but it is mostly accidental:

- Interviewers are people, with the accompanying social characteristics, e.g. age, gender, social class, ethnicity. For example, it may be possible to guess the social class of an interviewer from the way he/she speaks or dresses. Interviewers also have individual personalities, e.g. they may be shy or outgoing, caring or uncaring. The interviewee may react negatively to any of these characteristics and decide that he/she does not like the interviewer, thereby making it impossible to build up a relationship of trust.
- Some interviewees can be over-cooperative — in their eagerness to please the interviewer they may give him/her the replies they think he or she wants. This undermines validity.
- Interviewers may also unconsciously lead respondents into particular responses through their tone of voice or by their expression, e.g. one of approval or disapproval.
- In general, people like to present themselves to others in a positive light, and want to appear socially respectable. This social desirability effect may mean that respondents are open about those aspects of their behaviour that make them look like good citizens and conceal or lie about aspects on which they feel they will be judged negatively.
- However, sensitive subjects will produce exaggerated responses in particular groups. When questioned about sexual activities or numbers of friends, for example, research participants, especially young males, may exaggerate in order to impress the interviewer.

- Recording interviews can be problematic. Tape-recording ensures all the data are available for analysis, but may be inappropriate in some circumstances. Taking notes may act as a barrier between the researcher and the subjects and interrupt the relaxed nature of the interview.

Interviewing also depends on what people know about their own behaviour and the motives for it. This may be affected by faulty or hazy memory, but what if people do not recognise that they behave in a particular way? For example, if a researcher asks a police officer if he acts in a negative way towards black people, the officer would probably argue, in all innocence and sincerity, that he polices all people equally, regardless of social background. Some people may not know that they act in particular ways until they are shown clear evidence of it. Interviews will therefore uncover little about these people.

### Pilot interviews

It is important to carry out pilot interviews in order to iron out any potential problems with the interview schedule. Questions should be tested on a relatively small number of people, who share the characteristics of the main sample. A pilot study is useful because it can check that questions are clear and unambiguous, that they do not upset or lead the participants, that the sampling technique is successful, that the interviewers are well-trained and that the data produced are of the correct type. However, it is impossible to remove all potential problems completely.

**Key concepts**

interview bias or effect; non-response rate; pilot study; rapport; trust; focus interviews; group interviews; objectivity

## Observation

Some sociologists (interpretivists) are interested in understanding how people live their everyday lives. They argue that the research method of observation is the best possible way of understanding why people behave the way they do because it gives first-hand insight into how people interpret the social world around them. People can be observed in their natural environment and the sociologist can record their normal everyday behaviour. Research carried out in the natural environment of those being studied is known as 'ethnography'.

There are essentially two types of observation: non-participant observation and participant observation.

### Non-participant observation

Non-participant observation has been used extensively in the field of educational studies, and usually involves the researcher observing an activity such as a lesson. The researcher plays no active role. This type of observation often produces quantitative data, because the observer can count incidences of certain types of behaviour, e.g. how many times male students are disciplined by teachers compared with how many times female students are disciplined.

Supporters of this type of observation argue that because the researcher is detached and therefore objective, his or her interpretation of the group's behaviour is less likely to be biased. Moreover, because the researcher does not make any decisions or join in activities, the group itself will not be influenced by the observer. Critics of non-participant observation note that the observer is likely to observe artificial behaviour caused by his/her presence, and it gives little insight into the reasons why people behave in the way they do.

### Participant observation

Participant observation is the most common type of observation — the sociologist immerses him/herself in the lifestyle of the group being studied. These sociologists participate in the same activities as the group being researched and observe their everyday lives. The aim is to understand what is happening from the point of view of those involved; to 'get inside their heads' and to understand the meaning that they ascribe to their situation. The research, then, is naturalistic, i.e. it is carried out in the environment in which the respondents normally find themselves and is not based on the artificial situation created by an interview or questionnaire. The research may take months or even years.

Participant observation can be:
- overt — the researcher joins in the activities of a group, but some or all of the group know his or her identity; or
- covert or complete — the researcher conceals the fact that he/she is carrying out research, and pretends to be a member of the group

Successful participant observations depends on a number of factors:
- To gain entry to a group and be accepted by its members, researchers must share the social characteristics of the group being studied. Groups sometimes do not want to be studied, for example if they are engaged in illegal or deviant behaviour. Observation of these groups is likely to be covert, unless the researcher is sponsored by a trusted member of the group or can offer the group a service or role.
- Once the researcher gains entry, the focus should be on 'looking and listening', and going with the flow of social life. The researcher should not try to force the pace or interfere with 'normality'. The researcher should blend into the background until he/she has gained the trust of the group and his/her presence is taken for granted.
- Observation can be supplemented by questions, although if the researcher is carrying out covert research this might arouse suspicion and mistrust.
- Observers sometimes develop special relationships with key people within groups who can clarify the motives for particular behaviour.
- Much participant observation involves 'hanging around' — the research itself is often informal, unstructured and unplanned.
- Recording observations can be a problem in both overt and covert forms of observation. It is good for researchers to write up conversations while they are still fresh in their minds, but constantly taking notes can be off-putting to those who are

being observed. For researchers carrying out covert observation of a criminal or deviant group, writing notes, or disappearing for periods to do so, may arouse suspicion and put them in danger. However, most researchers keep a research diary as inconspicuously as possible.
- Observation can last months and years, and as such demands dedication.
- It can also be dangerous. The African-Caribbean sociologist Ken Pryce, who carried out a successful participant observation of St Pauls in Bristol, was murdered while attempting to carry out a participant observation study of organised crime.
- Observation can often lead to ethical dilemmas. Some observers have become involved in illegal activities in order to gain or retain the trust of the group. For example, Howard Parker's study of delinquents in Liverpool involved him keeping stolen property in his flat on behalf of the gang, and acting as look-out as they broke into cars.
- The researcher must eventually leave the group, which also raises ethical issues, especially in regard to covert observation. Is it right to pretend to be someone else and then use the friendships made in the group for research purposes? Could the published research get the group into trouble with the police? Is there any risk of harm, ridicule or reprisal to those identified by the researcher?

### Strengths of participant observation
- The researcher sees things through the eyes and actions of the group being studied, because he/she is in the same situation as the group's members and hopefully experiences fully what they are experiencing. This empathetic situation is known as *iverstehen*.
- Observation is high in validity because the sociologists can see what people do, as opposed to what they say they do when asked in questionnaires or interviews. The truth is therefore more likely to be observed and recorded.
- Observation can lead to unexpected findings that generate new insights. The sociologist might make observations that generate insights which he/she would not have had if questionnaires or interviews were used. Looking back on his observation of a street-corner gang in Boston, William Whyte noted 'As I sat and listened, I learned the answers to questions that I would not have had the sense to ask if I had been getting my information solely on an interviewing basis'.
- The sociologist gains a first-hand view, i.e. from 'the horse's mouth'. By watching and listening in the subject's natural environment, a participant observer has the chance to discover the priorities, concerns, anxieties and motivations that underpin the actions of those being studied.
- Participant observation often takes place over a long period of time, and therefore allows an understanding of how changes in attitudes and behaviour take place over months and years. Methods such as questionnaires and interviews can only give a snapshot picture, i.e. an understanding of the moment the questionnaire was filled in or on the day the interview was conducted.
- Observation may be the only practical method of researching hard-to-reach groups such as criminal gangs or religious sects, which may be hostile to conventional society.

### Weaknesses of participant observation

- The observer may become biased if he/she is too attached or sympathetic towards the group and 'go native', thereby losing detachment and objectivity, and identifying too closely with the group. The observer may then always interpret the behaviour of the group in a positive light, which will bias his/her analysis of the group's actions.
- The presence of the observer may result in the group acting less 'naturally', especially if its members are aware they are being studied. In Bill Whyte's study, the leader of the gang stated that he used to act on instinct, but now thought about how he was going to justify his actions to Whyte. Covert observation is less likely to lead to this effect.
- Some sociologists believe that covert observation breaks ethical rules, especially if informed consent has not been obtained. Researchers using covert observation have also been accused of abusing friendships. Some observers have taken part in illegal behaviour in order to reinforce the trust of the group being researched. Critics of covert observation argue that such behaviour can never be condoned in the interests of sociological research.
- Observation studies often suffer low reliability, because it is impossible to repeat the research and verify the data. The success of the research is often due to the unique personality of the sociologist and the exclusive relationships he or she has constructed. Another sociologist might find it impossible to gain the same degree of trust and rapport.
- The type of groups studied by observation are often not representative, because they are either exotic and therefore not typical of 'average' people (e.g. jazz musicians, members of the National Front), or the number of people observed is small. Consequently, it is often not possible to generalise from the findings of participant observation.
- The cost of observation studies in terms of time and money can be considerable.
- Recording data can be problematic. It is not usually possible to tape-record or write field notes during the observation, so researchers tend to rely on memory, which may be subjectively over-selective in support of a hypothesis, theory or political position.

#### Key concepts

covert observation; overt observation; participant observation; non-participant observation; *verstehen*; empathy; ethnographic

## Sources of secondary data

Secondary data are any data used by sociologists, which they did not collect for themselves. Such data include official statistics, personal or expressive documents such as diaries, letters, photographs, paintings and novels, public or official documents such as government reports and reports of other organisations such as companies, historical documents, mass media reports such as television, newspapers, magazines, the radio and the internet. The research of other sociologists and government bodies is often used as a starting point for researchers or as a point of comparison or reference for research.

### Personal documents

Personal documents are usually diaries, letters and other expressive documents. They can provide a sociologist with a rich source of qualitative data, and are often used to supplement quantitative secondary data, such as official statistics. For example, a diary or letters may be used to give meaning to public data on size of families, numbers of children and employment patterns, as when Valerie Hey used schoolgirls' notes as one method of researching friendships.

### Public documents

Public documents include government reports, reports of companies and reports from trade unions. They often provide a base upon which further research can be undertaken.

**Evaluation**

- The authenticity of documents, particularly historical documents, is often questioned. Are they genuine or not? Were they written by the person whom it is claimed wrote them?
- Is the material as accurate a portrayal of the events or issues as possible, or was it written to give a selective, prejudiced, partial and therefore biased view of some historical event? For example, the memoirs and letters of politicians may lack objectivity.
- Could the document(s) be said to be typical of material on the research subject?
- Are the authors representative of the social group to which they belong?
- To what extent is the meaning of the contents of the document(s) clear? Is it open to interpretation?
- Many expressive/personal documents provide detailed information not obtainable elsewhere, and increase the insights of researchers.

### Official statistics

Official statistics are produced by government departments. They cover all aspects of social life, such as crime, health, family life and education, and can be accessed via the internet or publications such as *Social Trends*.

The most commonly available source of official statistics is the census. This mass survey, last conducted in 2001, is carried out every tenth year on the whole population. Other government surveys include the General Household Survey, the Family Expenditure Survey and the Labour Force Survey.

Official statistics are cheap to access, cover a variety of sociologically relevant topics and are easily available. They have comparative value — past statistics can be compared with contemporary statistics to assess the success or failure of social policies.

- Official statistics may not present a complete picture — for example, crime statistics only cover reported crime.
- They may be used to put a particular political slant on an issue, and consequently may be biased. For example, governments frequently change the ways in which unemployment statistics are collected in order to make the situation look better than it is.
- Statistics are socially constructed — they tell us more about the priorities and interests of the people who collect them than about the social phenomena they are supposed to describe.
- Official statistics are not collected for sociological purposes, so their usefulness may be limited. Government officials may use different definitions, means of measurement and interpretations from those acceptable to sociologists.

**Key concepts**

secondary data; official government statistics; expressive documents; media reports; historical documents; authenticity; social construction

## Content analysis

Content analysis involves the detailed analysis of a form of the media, such as television advertising, women's magazines, newspapers and children's readers.

It requires the researcher to identify a set of categories that operationalise a research question or hypothesis in order to 'count' the number of times such categories occur. Using a systematic analysis of qualitative material, it results in quantitative data, and can be used as a comparative tool. For example, Best repeated Lobban's study of children's books in order to assess progress over 20 years.

Some types of content analysis involve a qualitative analysis of language, headlines, photographs etc., for example the Glasgow University Media Group's analysis of news.

Content analysis is generally regarded as a cheap and easily accessible means of research because mass media reports are readily available and there is no need to gather a representative sample audience for questionnaire or interview purposes.

**Evaluation**

- The reliability of content analysis has been questioned because the categories are determined by the researcher — different researchers may interpret such categories differently in terms of importance, impact on the audience etc.
- It can be a time-consuming method.
- The validity of research findings produced by content analysis has been questioned because data are selected according to the interpretations of the researcher, e.g. what one sociologist may see as a negative representation of women may be seen by another as a neutral or positive representation.
- Sociologists using content analysis often assume that media representations, content etc. have some effect on the audience, but this has never been proved convincingly.

### The internet

A recent trend is for research to be carried out over the internet. These projects tend to be questionnaire-based, but some are interview-based, and there has been some ethnographic research based on specific communities in cyberspace, e.g. entering chatrooms and 'observing' cyber-interaction.

#### Evaluation

- It is important to maintain a healthy scepticism towards the content of websites.
- Research using the internet means that the sample will be a self-selected group with the attendant problems of bias, although interviewer bias may be reduced.

# Multiple methods

Most sociologists today use a combination of techniques and data. You should be aware of the two most common approaches to combining research methods:

- Triangulation combines research methods in order to check or verify the validity and reliability of research findings. For example, a sociologist using participant observation might check the validity (i.e. truth) of his or her findings by asking the research subject(s) to fill in questionnaires, in order to make sure that he/she understood fully what was being observed. The sociologist might also ask subjects to keep a diary of their actions, which can be compared with the observation data.
- Methodological pluralism combines research methods in order to build up a fuller picture of what is being studied. Barker studied the 'Moonies' (the Unification Church). She conducted in-depth interviews, lived as a participant observer in several Moonie centres during the 6 years of her research, and constructed a 41-page questionnaire based on her findings from interviews and observation. This gave her a full and detailed picture, from several angles, about what being a Moonie entailed.

#### Evaluation

- Do not make the mistake of seeing triangulation as a method — it is an approach to collecting data that uses two or three methods.

Questions
&
Answers

T his section of the guide provides you with four questions on the topic of Exploring Socialisation, Culture and Identity in the style of the OCR examination. The first three questions are followed by grade-C candidate responses, which are on the right track but fail, for various reasons, to score very high marks. These are followed by grade-A responses to give you ideas about how to maximise your marks.

It is important to note that these are not 'model' answers. These responses are not the only possible answers to these questions, nor are they necessarily the best. They represent one particular successful style; one that answers the question set and demonstrates the appropriate skills, especially using suitable concepts and studies, displaying a critical and evaluative awareness towards the material used, and presenting a logically structured argument.

You must therefore not make the mistake of learning the A-grade responses parrot-fashion. Remember that you have to be flexible and able to respond to the specific demands of a question. It would be quite possible, particularly in the answers to (c) and (d), to take a different approach, or to use different material, or even to come to a different conclusion, and still gain very high marks.

A fourth question is provided which is not accompanied by a student answer. It is followed by a plan of action, and you should use this to write your own response. It is recommended that you spend some time revising the topic before tackling this question. You should answer the question under timed conditions with no notes.

## Examiner's comments

The candidate answers are accompanied by examiner's comments. These are preceded by the icon *e* and indicate where credit is due. For the grade-A answers, the examiner shows you what it is that enables the candidate to score so highly. Particular attention is given to the candidate's use of the examinable skills: knowledge and understanding; interpretation and analysis; and evaluation. For the grade-C answers, the examiner points out areas for improvement, specific problems and common errors.

# The formation and meaning of class identities

**Pre-release material: Charlesworth, S. (2000) *A Phenomenology of Working-Class Experience*, Cambridge University Press**

Simon Charlesworth comes from the town of Rotherham and is himself of working-class origin. Rotherham, in South Yorkshire, is one of the poorest regions in Europe. It is declining in economic and social terms. The work that is available is mainly casual and poorly paid. There are large numbers of members of ethnic minority communities. The centre of the town is decayed.

The purpose of the research was to give the poorest section of the Rotherham community a voice in which they could explain their feelings and points of view. Charlesworth also aimed to highlight the ways in which individuals are marked by their social class and the consequences for future opportunities, identities and 'style of being' for those stuck in the lowest and poorest strata of society. He hoped to gain some insight into the impact of poverty on the experience of ordinary working-class people.

He based his study on 43 interviews although in addition he spoke informally to large numbers of people he knew socially. He also observed them in their everyday environments. Two-thirds of his respondents were male. He also made a point of trying to talk to Asian members of the community. However Charlesworth has a tendency to be vague about those who took part in his interviews. He tells us little about them apart from their age and gender, and sometimes their economic status in the workforce. He does not clearly state the contexts in which the interviews took place or even their location.

The interviews were unstructured and conversational. The words of respondents are reported in an approximation of their Yorkshire dialect and pronunciation — a translation of some of the local terms is even included. Charlesworth sees the research as a two-way process — he is not merely recording the lives and language of his participants but attempting to open a dialogue with them so that they gave him an authentic and valid picture of their lives and feelings.

Charlesworth was able 'to speak the language' because he was familiar with the community and people knew him as a local person rather than just as an academic outsider. He deliberately framed his questions in order to seem naïve to his respondents. This was in order to encourage respondents to elaborate and talk about themselves and their views. There was a danger in this — it made him seem stupid sometimes and embarrassed the respondents.

It was also necessary for him to memorise conversations and note them later. People were sometimes reluctant to answer even in informal situations like the gym. Charlesworth also found it difficult to explain the meaning and purpose of his work to some of his respondents. Even some of his closest friends would not allow themselves to be interviewed.

Charlesworth found that social class and the experience of poverty permeated all aspects of life in Rotherham and the lives of people suffered as a consequence. The loss of a man's job, for example, had an objective physical consequence because it produced fear and panic due to loss of earnings and a sense of unpredictability. Charlesworth found that miserable economic conditions cause people to feel both physically and psychologically unhealthy.

Many unemployed working-class people in Charlesworth's study experienced a lack of identity and felt that they were no longer valued by society. He claimed that working-class children learned the basic 'truths of class inequality' at an early age. They learned that to be working class meant low status, disrespect and helplessness.

Charlesworth claimed that working-class life was characterised by insecurity — of work, of health and of opportunities. Changes in the social climate left people without a sense of belonging or of understanding how the world was developing. They had little sense of hope for the future and worried for their children. Many found it difficult to make social connections and nearly all felt a breakdown in community.

(a) **Define the concept of subculture. Illustrate your answer with examples.** (8 marks)

(b) **Outline and explain how any two agents of socialisation influence how girls learn how to be feminine.** (16 marks)

(c) **Explain and briefly evaluate why some sociologists believe that social class is still the main influence on identity in the UK today.** (24 marks)

(d) **Using the pre-release material and your wider sociological knowledge, explain the use of ethnographic methods to research the experience of working-class people in Rotherham.** (52 marks)

■ ■ ■

## Answer to question 1: grade-C candidate

**(a)** A subculture is a minority group that exists within wider society which has its own way of doing things and its own beliefs, which might be different from those of the majority. For example, young people sometimes belong to groups of punks or Goths, who like to dress differently from 'normal' members of society. Society often defines such groups as deviant.

🖉 The definition of 'subculture' is satisfactory — subcultures tend to be minority groups and the candidate touches on the concept of the group having its own unique norms ('way of doing things') and value system ('own beliefs'). There is also a reference to 'difference' and deviance, although reasons for this difference are unexplained. The example, however, is lacking in development — it does not contribute much to our understanding of the concept of subculture, apart from the vague notion of young people dressing differently from the rest of society, and better examples were available. This candidate gains 5 marks out of a possible 8.

**(b)** The family is a huge influence on femininity. Parents are responsible for gender role socialisation. Oakley argues that parents teach girls how to be female by buying them feminine toys and games, e.g. dolls are still a popular present for girls. These teach girls that they are expected to have maternal and domestic skills when they get older — they are taught to be mothers and housewives. Children also copy their parents when playing, so boys are more likely to play at being a worker, while girls are more likely to copy their mother.

🖉 This paragraph successfully identifies the 'family' as an agent of gender role social-isation, and the reference to Oakley is accurate. However, it lacks sociological character and consequently has an anecdotal feel, because it fails to highlight soci-ological concepts such as canalisation, manipulation, imitation, hegemonic masculinity and femininity. Oakley's work is also more sophisticated than the candidate implies.

Another major influence on femininity is the mass media. Advertising, for example, reinforces traditional ideas about femininity. On television commercials, women are still the main target audience for selling domestic products and it is assumed without question that they should be mainly responsible for cleaning, cooking, looking after the kids, shopping, washing etc. Younger women are portrayed as sexy and thin. They are encouraged to worry about getting fat, wrinkly, and old. Tabloid newspapers also criticise stars such as Kate Winslet if they put on weight (although Victoria Beckham is criticised for being too thin). However, the idea that slimness equals happiness dominates media coverage of women.

🖉 This paragraph makes more sophisticated points than the previous one, but the lack of empirical evidence in the form of studies lets it down.

Newspapers rarely celebrate women for their achievements in education and work. The emphasis is nearly always on looking sexy or being someone's wife or girlfriend. Women's magazines also reinforce traditional ideas about femininity. As Ferguson argues, women's magazines such as *Woman's Own* are like appren-tice manuals for being good wives and mothers.

🖉 The point about newspapers is valid, but the candidate again fails to support it with reference to sociological evidence and studies. The final reference to Ferguson is

a good one but it lacks depth and detail — illustration is needed to explain how such magazines act as apprentice manuals for women.

📝 **Overall this candidate demonstrates some satisfactory knowledge of gender role socialisation, although the material on the media is better than that on the family. However, the lack of empirical studies, reference to concepts and illustration mean that this candidate only demonstrates basic skills overall and gains 6 out of 12 marks for knowledge and understanding. The interpretation, particularly of the role of media, deserves greater reward and consequently gains 3 out of a possible 4 marks.**

**(c)** It is said today that social class is no longer the most important source of an individual's identity. Some sociologists, especially postmodernists, think that society is becoming classless. It is said that the media and our consumer culture now provide us with all the identity we need and therefore traditional influences like social class and community are less important in people's lives. However, other sociologists like Marshall argue that class identity is still the main influence on identity in the UK today.

📝 This introduction sets the scene for the debate and identifies two competing positions (postmodernism and Marshall).

Some sociologists argue that certain jobs are likely to result in a greater sense of class identity than others. Manual work, and mining in particular, is often dangerous and workers think of themselves as a community that should stick together through thick and thin. As a result, miners are very proud to be working class. Factory workers were also traditionally proud to be working class because they worked alongside hundreds of other workers, and as a result they felt a strong sense of identification with each other. Trade union membership in factory work was high for similar reasons.

📝 The candidate fails to mention any studies in this section. This is disappointing, because the points raised are valid but they are undermined by their anecdotal character.

Middle-class people are less likely to have developed a class identity, according to studies by Roberts, Savage etc. However, they do have a common culture with distinct values and norms, e.g. 'keeping up with the Joneses', an obsession with respectability and decency. Savage argues that middle-class professionals pass on these values to their children, and that this is why they do well in education. He calls this 'cultural capital'. Middle-class professionals also use their economic capital — their superior income — to support their children educationally.

📝 This paragraph is an improvement on the previous one. The point about middle-class identity is referenced accurately. The candidate uses the concept of common culture well, but is less successful in using the concept of cultural capital — this requires further illustration.

Some sociologists have focused on how being working class may affect working-class youth identity. Williams found that working-class youth saw football hooliganism as attractive because it allowed them the opportunity to exaggerate working-class values by being seen to be tough, strong and hard. Jefferson found a similar attitude among skinheads in the 1970s. They dressed in a working-class fashion with Doc Martens, braces etc. in order to celebrate their working-class roots. Willis also showed how working-class boys rejected school values in favour of their own class values.

> This is an excellent paragraph that makes valid points about how youth might interpret working-class identity. The studies are used in an excellent manner. This is a good example of applied sociology.

However, it is important to note that class may no longer be the main influence on people's identity in the UK. Devine found that being working class was less important than family life for factory workers today in Luton. Ethnic minorities may see their culture or religion as more important. Jacobson's study found that Pakistani youth believed being Islamic to be more important than being working class.

> This section is focused on the question and evaluative. It makes an excellent point about the new working class, and culture and religion as alternative sources of identity for young Pakistanis, and illustrates with good examples of empirical studies.

Other sociologists have focused on how the poor and unemployed view themselves. There is some evidence that these people feel society does not treat them fairly. Charlesworth found that the poor in Rotherham did not think much about their working-class identity because they were too busy attempting to get by. He found that the poor were psychologically and physically unhealthy. Class was therefore something that brought about misery in Rotherham.

> This paragraph links poverty to social class by using the pre-release material. However, while the points made are relevant, the candidate makes no reference to a lot of useful material that could have been used to illustrate the argument further.

Finally, some sociologists say class is dead or that it is no longer important. It is said that in modern societies we get our identity from the media and popular culture.

> This paragraph has the potential for evaluation, but fails to develop either of the two points made. In particular, the reference to media and popular culture is too vague. The candidate needs to explain how people get their identity from these sources.

> **This is a good response. It displays a sound knowledge and understanding of the debate, although it is a little unbalanced. It would benefit from more detail in the points about ethnicity, religion and particularly the postmodern view on media and popular culture. However, the**

candidate deals with concepts well throughout and uses empirical studies confidently to support his/her case. The candidate therefore gains 7 out of 12 marks for knowledge and understanding. In terms of interpretation and analysis, the candidate focuses on the debate and applies a range of ideas, concepts and studies to it — he/she gains 5 marks out of 8 for these skills. Alternatives to class are offered, but there should be more explicit evaluation of these options, especially with regard to the role of popular culture and the media. The candidate gains 2 out of 4 marks for evaluation, making a total of 14 marks out of 24.

**(d)** Ethnographic methods refer to research methods used in the natural everyday places in which the group being studied go (e.g. observation), or conducted in places in which they feel safe and comfortable (e.g. unstructured interviews) Unstructured interviews are like conversations — they are not formal and therefore people believe that what they are saying is important. This encourages respondents to say things they wouldn't normally say in a structured interview or in response to a questionnaire.

> The candidate has touched on the core meaning of ethnography (i.e. research carried out in the everyday natural environment of those being studied), and successfully identified two ethnographic methods — observation and unstructured interviews. A good comparative point is made about interviews.

Charlesworth used ethnographic methods in the area of Rotherham where he grew up and with people who knew him socially. During the period of his research, he moved back into the area and looked up old friends. This didn't always work, as some of his friends were embarrassed about their poverty and refused to speak to him about it. He conducted 43 unstructured interviews with people living on the council estate he grew up on and observed people in the pub. He also had conversations with people, which he secretly wrote down.

> This is a good summary of Charlesworth's research design, although the candidate should refrain from evaluating Charlesworth before the appropriate part of his/her answer.

His interviews were mainly with men, so his sample was not very representative of the community. He also did not talk to many Asians or black people. Therefore he could not generalise to other poor communities.

> This paragraph makes good references to the concepts of 'representativeness' and 'generalisability'.

It is not clear how Charlesworth chose the people he interviewed or whether they were told the purpose of the research. If he didn't tell them, then he was breaking ethical rules.

> This is a reasonable reference to ethical problems, although it would benefit from more detail.

Charlesworth used unstructured interviews — he did not use a questionnaire. He probably had a list of general questions, but these would have been flexible. If a person had said something really interesting, Charlesworth would have let them have their say and asked them follow-up questions. Some sociologists don't like this — they say it is unreliable because people do not get the same questions. These interviews are almost impossible to repeat for other sociologists who want to check that the people involved in the research really felt that way.

> 🖉 This is a brief but accurate discussion of the merits of unstructured interviews — it would be better if the candidate identified the types of sociologist that do not like unstructured interviews. This paragraph includes a good reference to reliability.

A big problem with interviews is interviewer bias. The social characteristics of an interviewer — his/her class, sex, age etc. — can put people off answering because they feel threatened or believe that the interviewer might use the information against them. In Rotherham, people might have been put off by Charlesworth's status as a university professor.

> 🖉 These points are all valid ones to make about interviewer bias, but lack of detail lets the paragraph down. The examiner should not have to ask 'how?' or 'why?' about a candidate's answer.

Another problem is that people might want to please Charlesworth, especially if they knew him. If they know he is researching poverty, they may exaggerate their stories of misery to give him what he wants.

> 🖉 The reference to the 'social desirability effect' is good, but the paragraph is superficial. If the candidate had linked the concept of 'validity' to these points, more marks would have been gained.

Finally, Charlesworth used observation to back up his interviews. He spent a lot of time watching people in the pub and betting shop. However, it is difficult to tell how people are feeling from just watching them and he may have misinterpreted their behaviour — just because people look sad, it doesn't mean they are.

> 🖉 The candidate misses an opportunity in terms of discussing the merits of participant observation here. It is a vague paragraph that makes only generalised points about this research method.

> 🖉 **On the whole, this response, although good on Charlesworth's use of unstructured interviews, lacks depth and detail. The candidate misses many potential evaluative points about the practical side of Charlesworth's research which were apparent in the pre-release material, e.g. his use of observation. The candidate therefore needs to make better use of the preparatory period between receiving the pre-release material and the examination. This candidate gains 13 marks for knowledge and understanding — he/she demonstrates a good grasp of unstructured interviews. The candidate gains 7 marks for interpretation**

and application — illustrative detail is largely missing. He/she gains 12 marks for evaluation and analysis — the use of unstructured interviews is assessed well, although the lack of detail lets the response down. In total, this candidate gains 32 marks out of a possible 52.

This candidate scored 60 marks out of 100 for question 1.

■ ■ ■

## Answer to question 1: grade-A candidate

**(a)** The concept of subculture refers to the existence of minority cultures that exist alongside mainstream society or culture. Usually such groups share most of the values and norms of the greater society, but may support some norms and values that are unique to them. For example, ethnic minorities such as British-born Pakistanis may subscribe to British culture in most respects, e.g. they believe in educational achievement, but their everyday lives may also be influenced by the religious system of Islam in terms of how they dress, their leisure activities etc.

Some sociologists have suggested that anti-school and deviant street subcultures may be responsible for boys' underachievement in the UK. For example, Sewell sees male African-Caribbean underachievement at school as caused partly by deviant subcultural activity which values masculinity over academic success. Other sociologists, especially Marxists, have focused on the emergence of deviant youth subcultures such as teddy boys, mods, rockers, skinheads and punks, and argue that these groups are temporarily opposed to mainstream adult society and symbolic of a generation gap.

⌨ **This is a sophisticated definition because it is constructed around explicit sociological concepts such as culture, values and norms. The example used is excellent — it shows how subcultures are part of and yet set apart from mainstream culture. The candidate also makes a good reference to how sociologists including Sewell and Marxists have used the concept of subculture to explain anti-school, street and youth subcultures. This answer gains the full 8 marks.**

**(b)** It is important to understand that there are different types of femininity in the UK. According to Tunstall, females have traditionally been seen as best suited to the roles of domestic goddess, home-maker, wife, romantic, shopper-consumer, mother and emotional caretaker. Generally, the function of gender role socialisation was to prepare girls to accept adult futures in which they would defer to men and be content to take on the main responsibility for these traditional domestic roles.

⌨ Most candidates tend to take a narrow view of femininity and focus only on its traditional aspects, but this candidate realises that it is a fluid concept, with different versions as a consequence. The reference to Tunstall is excellent.

The role of the family as an agent of gender role socialisation is to socially construct male and female identity by training girls and boys to behave and think in feminine and masculine ways. Oakley identifies two aspects of gender role socialisation in the family which are central to reinforcing traditional divisions and identities. First, she focuses on 'manipulation', i.e. the way in which parents encourage or discourage gender appropriate behaviour in children. For example, boys may be discouraged from being emotional, while boyish behaviour may be tolerated in a female child until adolescence. Lake found that mothers tend to be more emotional with female children and fuss over their appearance more than with boys. Second, Oakley identifies 'canalisation', which refers to the way parents channel their children's interests into toys and activities that are gender appropriate. For example, parents tend to give girls toys which are a preparation for motherhood and domesticity and may encourage them to assist with domestic tasks.

🖉 This paragraph shows an excellent use of concepts such as social construction, manipulation and canalisation, linked explicitly to traditional ideas about femininity. There is accurate and detailed use of Oakley.

However, new types of femininity have appeared in recent years, symbolised by the fact that many young women today are not following traditional gender paths. It can be argued that changes in the way education socialises girls has led to a major change in the social expectations associated with femininity. Today, female achievement at all levels of the examination system outstrips that of males. Consequently, according to Sharpe, this positive experience of education means that girls are now more interested in gaining qualifications, a career and economic independence from men. Marriage and motherhood, although not dismissed altogether, are now low on their list of priorities. Wilkinson argues that the change in attitude among young women is now so radically different from previous generations that it constitutes a 'genderquake'.

🖉 **The second agency of socialisation is linked convincingly to a new aspirational version of femininity, using empirical studies such as Sharpe and Wilkinson. This is the work of a confident candidate. This answer gains full marks — 12 marks for knowledge and understanding and 4 marks for interpretation and application.**

(c) It can be argued that people's identities are the product of the type of work they do and the occupational subcultures to which they belong. Sociologists use jobs to categorise people into social classes. Evidence suggests that our class position and resulting identity may shape our behaviour in regard to education, health, leisure and lifestyle.

🖉 This is a good introduction, focusing on making clear the importance of social class to people's sense of identity. However, it is somewhat assertive, and should be supported by sociological data or evidence.

If we examine the working class, we can see three distinct types of working-class identity. First, Parkin identifies a deferential working class largely made up of rural workers, who believe that the world has a natural hierarchy and those at the top (i.e. their employers) are somehow born to rule.

> The candidate identifies a social group whose culture is influenced by the nature of its class relationships with others. Concepts like values and ascribed status are used accurately. The points made are referenced clearly to a valid sociological study.

Second, studies of traditional working-class communities, such as 'Coal Is Our Life' by Dennis, Henriques and Slaughter, suggest that manual workers like miners have a strong sense of their class position. Working-class culture is community-based — workers feel a strong sense of loyalty and obligation to each other and see themselves as a distinct group in conflict with employers and managers. This sense of 'them' versus 'us' is reflected in mass membership of trade unions, voting for the political party which represents their class interests (the old Labour Party) and a mutual support system underpinned by close relationships with extended kin. Paul Willis's work on factory life identifies physical bravery and strength, masculinity and skills gained through experience as typical working-class values, rather than education.

> This is an excellent section, demonstrating a range of knowledge about working-class culture and the role of social class. Two sociological studies are referenced in a convincing fashion.

Some commentators have noted that such communities are in decline, because the numbers employed in traditional industries such as mining and shipbuilding have fallen considerably. Therefore, it is argued that this type of class identity, which Goldthorpe called 'proletarian traditionalist', is in decline because its economic basis (i.e. manual work) has weakened.

> The candidate uses an evaluative tone successfully.

Third, research has identified a 'new' form of working class. Devine's research indicated that workers of this type do not see work as the defining feature of their life. Rather, they see work as a means to an end. This type of worker is instrumentalist in attitude, i.e. work is not expected to be satisfying but merely a means of providing a standard of living. Family, consumption and lifestyle shape the workers' identity. Consequently, they have no heightened sense of class awareness, loyalty or political allegiance.

> The candidate focuses on the central argument in the question and challenges it by referring to a third type of 'working class', in which class identity is not a priority.

Charlesworth's study of a deprived working-class community in Rotherham has also suggested that class identity is in decline. Many of the unemployed in his study expressed little interest in their working-class identity. Many of them felt that this identity had done nothing for them, because the poverty they experienced meant that they were no longer valued by society. Charlesworth claimed that children in his study learnt that being working class meant learning basic 'truths' such as low status, disrespect and helplessness. Furthermore, being working class meant experiencing little hope for one's children, and anxiety about how these children would get on in the future. There was little sense of working-class community, belonging or mutual support on the estate that Charlesworth investigated, compared with traditional working-class communities.

☑ This is an excellent interpretation of Charlesworth's work, which is integrated well into the general argument.

In addition to research into working-class identity, research has also uncovered a range of different types of middle-class identity. Savage notes some key cultural differences between professionals whose culture values knowledge, qualifications and the passing on of cultural capital to their children, and managers whose culture values standard of living and leisure pursuits. Studies of upper-class identity suggest that members of this class also have a powerful sense of identity, which, according to Scott, is reinforced by private schooling and an old-boy network.

☑ The candidate takes the discussion beyond working-class identity and examines other social class groups. There is so much information to access that the candidate has made the decision to spend less time on these groups. This is sensible, because he/she has only 25 minutes to answer this question. Most of the material in this section is an optional extra, although a good response will always make some brief reference to both the upper and middle classes.

In recent years, some sociologists have argued that these class identities are becoming less important, because both the economy and society have changed radically. In particular, the decline in manufacturing and the increase in service sector jobs, such as call centre operatives, have allegedly changed the nature of work so that workers no longer look to their jobs for satisfaction or identity. People are increasingly looking for identity outside occupation and class. Postmodern identity is more likely to be influenced by popular culture and the diversity and choice that characterises mass consumption. The search for style through brands and logos is said to be the main influence on young people's identity today.

☑ This candidate understands that to 'discuss' means to evaluate the argument that class is central to identity in the 'contemporary' UK. The reference to theory, although not compulsory, is accurate and there is a clear explanation of why class identity might have been replaced by identity based on consumption.

Other sociologists note that feminine identity has become more important in recent years because of increasing opportunities in the job market. Sociologists such as Mason note that ethnic minority subcultures may see their identity wrapped up in their culture and religion, especially if the majority culture discriminates against them.

📝 Good points are made here about the importance of gender and ethnicity as sources of identity.

Finally, some sociologists argue that these ideas about consumption are exaggerated. They point out that consumption and style are superficial and temporary indicators of identity. Marshall's survey indicates that many manual workers still see social class as the most important influence in their lives. Marshall argues that class has not declined in importance, and people still use it to judge others, alongside gender, age and ethnic identities. He also criticises postmodernists for neglecting the fact that consumption is dependent on having a job and an income.

📝 This is a good conclusion, using empirical evidence to take the evaluation one step further, i.e. by evaluating the consumption argument.

📝 **The candidate's answer to part (c) demonstrates an excellent level and range of conceptual and empirical knowledge, and he/she gains the full 12 marks for knowledge and understanding. In addition, the candidate sustains an analysis and debate consistently and the key question is addressed throughout. He/she therefore gains 8 marks for interpretation and analysis. Evaluation is focused in a balanced way on all sides of the argument, gaining 4 marks. The candidate gains the full 24 marks for this part of the question.**

(d) Ethnography is sociological research conducted in the natural environment of the research subjects, which aims to describe their way of life. It generally intends to give research subjects a voice, so data are often composed of qualitative extracts from conversations or interviews, thus allowing the data to speak for themselves.

📝 This is an excellent and focused definition of ethnography.

Charlesworth's research was ethnographic — he spent a great deal of time in an economically deprived area (Rotherham) and aimed to give the poorest section of that community a platform from which they could describe and explain how they felt about living in poverty. Charlesworth was mainly concerned with validity — getting an authentic picture of how people experienced poverty. His research methods were ethnographic in the sense that he lived among the community during the research period and was able to observe people informally in their everyday environment. He also conducted 43 unstructured interviews with residents, and had informal conversations with dozens of people he already knew from school etc. in the pub and betting shop.

📝 The candidate accurately contextualises Charlesworth's research as ethnographic and links this convincingly to the concept of validity. There is also an excellent summary of his research approach.

Charlesworth's research is essentially interpretivist, because he aimed to get inside the heads of his respondents and to experience the world of Rotherham from their point of view — he aimed to achieve *verstehen*, or empathetic understanding. He wished to see if people living in this area shared similar interpretations of their poverty and social class experience.

*e* The candidate makes an excellent link to the theoretical reasons for Charlesworth's approach to research. Note the use of the concept of *verstehen*.

Charlesworth generally used unstructured interviews — 43 official interviews and a number of informal conversations. He does not state whether the interviews were recorded, although the fact that the words of respondents were reported in Rotherham dialect indicates a formal recording process in the official interviews.

*e* The candidate engages with the practical side of the research.

The informal conversations carried out in the street, pub, betting shop etc. were more problematic because people did not realise he was interviewing them. Ethical concerns could be raised here because Charlesworth did not seek informed consent. He had to make notes about these conversations in secret, memorise conversations and write up his notes after the conversations. This type of situation always creates problems of validity because it takes an exceptional memory to recall every word of a conversation correctly, and it is likely that what Charlesworth recalled was his own interpretation of what was said. He may have misrepresented some of his respondents.

*e* Excellent points are made about the ethical side of the research, and issues of validity are raised.

Charlesworth certainly misled some of his respondents, and he could be accused of using and abusing friendship in order to obtain sociological data. However, the secretive measures might be justified by the fact that people were reluctant to speak formally about their situation.

*e* This paragraph raises more excellent points about the ethics of the study.

Another problem in Charlesworth's use of interviews was that it was unclear how people were sampled. There are no signs that he used a sampling frame or a random sampling technique, and bias can become a problem if a sample is not randomly selected. If Charlesworth used a non-random sampling technique, such as snowball sampling, he might have been using an unrepresentative or atypical sample. Charlesworth's discussion of his research can be criticised for its vagueness in this respect. He tells us little about his respondents apart from their age and gender, and occasionally whether they are employed or not. It is unclear how many of his respondents were black or Asian. It is not even clear where the interviews took place or how they were physically organised. All these factors make it difficult to assess the validity of the data gathered.

*e* Sampling and access to the group are areas of the research that must be discussed. This is an excellent summary of the concerns about Charlesworth's access to the group being studied.

**question**

We know that Charlesworth used unstructured interviews, which have some strengths. They allow the researcher to establish a relationship with the respondent, because they generally place the respondent at the centre of the interview. Interviewees feel that they have greater control over the direction of the interview and consequently talk about what they feel, rather than what the interviewer feels is important, making them more likely to open up. These characteristics of the unstructured interview increase the respondent's trust in the interviewer, which generates more validity, in terms of richer, vivid and colourful data. Charlesworth states that this was his intention — he wanted the research to be a two-way process (a dialogue) in which the lives and language of the people of Rotherham could be recorded faithfully and authentically.

✍ This paragraph links a sociological discussion of the merits of unstructured interviews convincingly to Charlesworth's research.

However, Charlesworth may have had problems using unstructured interviews. They are time consuming, difficult to transcribe and analyse because of the sheer volume of material in the respondents' own words. Positivists would not be keen on Charlesworth's methods because such interviews depend on a unique relationship between the interviewer and interviewee that cannot be repeated and checked. There are also doubts about the objectivity of such interviews, as Charlesworth may have selectively quoted or interpreted material based on his own experience of living in the community.

✍ This discussion is focused on Charlesworth. Although it is easy to learn the strengths and weaknesses of particular methods, the real skill is linking it to the practical research, which this candidate does well.

The biggest problem with such interviews is interviewer effect or bias. Asian people may have been put off by Charlesworth's personal characteristics, e.g. by the fact that he is white. Some of his closest friends refused to be interviewed. However, Charlesworth claims that by presenting himself as a local guy with a local accent, rather than as an academic, this encouraged respondents to elaborate and talk about themselves. He also presented himself as naïve and asked simplistic questions, although he admits that he probably sounded stupid and that this may have embarrassed and put off his respondents.

✍ This is a good summary of interviewer effect, located in the context of Charlesworth's research.

There was also the danger of the social desirability effect — people may have wanted to please Charlesworth, or to present themselves as socially respectable. Consequently, they may have concealed or lied about aspects of their experience, therefore undermining validity. Finally, people are sometimes unaware that they are behaving in a particular way — interviews will not pick up this information.

✍ The social desirability effect is linked to the validity of Charlesworth's data in a convincing fashion.

Charlesworth used informal observation to compensate for the weaknesses of interviews. This is participant observation — Charlesworth attempted to immerse himself in the lifestyle of Rotherham people by living among them and hanging around the pub, the betting shop etc. He hoped that this would give him an extra angle by helping him to understand the meanings that the participants gave to their poverty-stricken situation, and to give him insights into their physical and psychological situation. His use of observation therefore gave him a first-hand insider's view of poverty and added to the overall validity of the study.

📝 The candidate recognises the importance of observation as an ethnographic tool and links it well to the aims of Charlesworth's research.

There are drawbacks to using informal observation — Charlesworth might have 'gone native' and identified too closely with the residents, many of whom were his friends. Many of them probably knew he was an academic, and they may have acted less naturally in his presence. The data produced by observation cannot be checked and therefore are seen by some as unreliable.

📝 This is an excellent discussion of problems that Charlesworth might have experienced.

Overall, Charlesworth's study is a good example of interpretivist research using methods that often produce rich valid data, giving insight into how people feel about their situation. However, as with all studies that cannot be repeated, there may be some doubts about the reliability and objectivity of the study.

📝 This a good summary of the merits of Charlesworth's research, which is worth doing if you have the time.

📝 **This is an excellent response, which is focused on Charlesworth's research throughout. This candidate knows and understands both the theoretical and practical strengths and problems of using unstructured interviews and observation as research tools. The candidate is also focused on problems relating to ethics, access and sampling. This candidate gains 20 marks for knowledge and understanding, 12 marks for interpretation and application, and 20 marks for evaluation and analysis, i.e. the full 52 marks available. It is difficult to envisage a better response.**

**This candidate gains the full 100 marks for question 1.**

# The formation and meaning of gender identities

**Pre-release material: Hey,V. (1997)** *The Company She Keeps: An Ethnography of Girls' Friendships,* **Open University Press**

The study was written within the context of feminist sociology and concerns an ethnographic study of girls and their friendships in two London comprehensive schools. The study was an attempt to provide a first-hand account using participant observation of female emotional dynamics. The aims were fourfold; first, to investigate how girls create their identities through talking and writing; second, to gain an understanding of the processes that take place in girls' social networks; third, to recognise how females negotiate their relationships with an outside world that is male-dominated; and fourth, to investigate the ways that girls create intensely pleasurable, emotional 'lived' personal lives in the face of male repression.

Hey's methods were highly organised but she was flexible enough to adapt to changing circumstances. Some of the techniques that she used were developed while the research was in progress as a result of a significant incident or a sudden insight. She also refers to some of the issues that arose from being a female researcher conducting a study in a school in which gender inequality was a sensitive issue.

Most of the research was carried out in 'Crossfield', a small single-sex school in a working-class area. Hey offers a detailed account of the procedures and sources of information that she used. These were varied and imaginative. She is open about her own inexperience and relates stories about situations where her misunderstanding exposed her to ridicule and embarrassment. She was also in the awkward position of being older than the girls. Although she is an ex-teacher, she was still a stranger attempting to penetrate an intimate and private set of relationships.

Hey experienced some difficulty in penetrating her target groups and worked in the closest details with girls of a younger age than she originally intended. This meant that she was unable to penetrate Asian and black friendship groups.

Hey spent her time with girls doing what they were doing: attending lessons, going on cross-country runs and even truanting! The girls tested Hey to see whether she would tell their teachers of their misbehaviour. Hey is open about the fact that there was a trading situation occurring. She would exchange small gifts of time, sometimes money, excuses to miss lessons, attention and advice in return for access to information about the girls' social lives and emotions. Hey, as a result of her experience, suggests that ethnographic research requires considerable ethical compromise that is often denied or avoided in subsequent accounts by researchers.

Hey made friends with girls, and sometimes these relationships were fairly close so that the girls were able to explain the meanings of their slang and the social context in which exchanges were occurring. One particular study group of working-class girls (led by Jude) were frequent truants and so Hey necessarily spent time with them outside school.

One of her main sources of data was provided by the notes that girls wrote to each other in class. She collected a wide variety of these and was given examples by sympathetic staff. Girls gave her examples of notes that had been saved for long periods of time, years in some cases.

Hey found that girls often need to keep their friendships with each other invisible. Girls use strategies to keep their emotional discussions and negotiations private and this includes the practice of note-writing. Girls tend to group together with other girls from the same social class. These cliques involve a core of best friends and others who move in and out of favour with the core group.

She also found that girls are constantly involved in complex judgemental processes and part of the power of a group is represented by the ability to exclude individuals from intimacy. Girls may misread their emotional connections, so that one could describe another as 'best friend' whereas in response the other girl sees the same relationship as 'casual'.

Hey found that girls use insults to exclude girls from the group based on relative physical attractiveness, e.g. 'flatchested' or her perceived morality, e.g. 'she's a slapper'. She also found that girls use heterosexuality as a means of control in a patriarchal environment in which girls are relatively powerless. They use their bodies to attract and control men. The ultimate control was being attractive to boys without having to do 'it'.

(a) **Define the concept of cultural diversity. Illustrate your answer with examples.** (8 marks)

(b) **Outline and explain how any two agents of socialisation influence traditional working-class identity.** (16 marks)

(c) **Explain and briefly evaluate the view that the dominant values and norms associated with femininity today are very different from those held by previous generations.** (24 marks)

(d) **Using the pre-release material and your wider sociological knowledge, explain the use of participant observation to research how teenage girls create their identities.** (52 marks)

■ ■ ■

## Answer to question 2: grade-C candidate

**(a)** Cultural diversity refers to the fact that British society is no longer a totally white society. About 8% of British society is made up of people who belong to ethnic minorities. However, the continued existence of racism means that not everybody is happy with the idea of cultural diversity.

> ✐ **The candidate has defined cultural diversity in an appropriate fashion and used an accurate statistic to illustrate it. However, he/she should have developed the illustration further, e.g. by discussing which groups make up the 8%, why 'not everybody is happy' with cultural diversity, or by identifying the different theoretical perspectives on cultural diversity. The candidate gains 4 marks for knowledge and understanding of the concept.**

**(b)** Traditional working-class identity refers to how manual workers who worked in traditional industries viewed themselves. People like miners and factory workers were often proud to call themselves working class because of their employment situation. Many of their values and beliefs about being working class were learnt at work. This was because they felt close to other workers — either their jobs were dangerous (and therefore they depended on other workers for their safety) or they worked in factories which employed hundreds, if not thousands, of other workers. They therefore felt a strong sense of community, which was reinforced by member-ship of trade unions and strikes.

> ✐ This is a good summary of the characteristics of working-class identity and how it is shaped by the workplace or 'employment situation'. However, it needs an empirical base — no sociological studies are cited in support.

Another major influence on the identity of working-class people was their home and community life. According to Wilmott and Young, working-class people lived in close-knit communities because the men worked at the same place. Families were often extended; sons worked alongside their fathers in the mines and facto-ries, and daughters saw their mothers on most days. There was a mutual support system in that people helped each other out with babysitting or lending money. They also socialised with each other in pubs and working-men's clubs.

> ✐ **This is a successful summary of how the family, as an agent of socialisa-tion, influences working-class identity — it is detailed, and it cites an appropriate study. This answer to part (b) gains 8 marks for knowledge and understanding and 3 marks for interpretation and application.**

**(c)** In my view, there are a variety of different types of femininity in Britain today. Girls are no longer committed just to getting married and having children. Their attitudes and beliefs are very different from those of their mothers and grandmothers. Young females no longer want to follow their mothers into marriage and motherhood; they want more out of life, including careers and financial independence.

✐ This introduction is assertive, and reads like the student's opinion or something he/she read in a newspaper. It lacks sociological grounding in terms of data or reference to studies such as those by Sue Sharpe and Helen Wilkinson.

There is evidence for this. Chandler talks about an increase in voluntary child-lessness, and the latest household statistics show that the number of single-person households has increased in recent years. Much of this increase is among young females.

✐ This section is a distinct improvement. The reference to Chandler is good and there is a reference to a valid social trend.

Even among married women, we can see that traditional ideas about women being mothers and housewives, and putting up with men ordering them about, are being abandoned. More and more women are going out to work and insisting that men share the housework and the childcare. There is evidence too that women are using divorce more than men to gain their independence. One reason for this is that our attitude towards femininity has changed and we no longer condemn single mothers.

✐ The candidate reverts to assertion again, which is a shame because sociological analysis is introduced in this paragraph. For example, the points about women going out to work and more women suing for divorce are valid, although the link to new femininities is not clear and the points are not backed up with any evidence in the form of data or studies. The final sentence in this paragraph is also contentious.

There is also evidence that girls are becoming more like men. Celebrities like Kate Moss, Amy Winehouse and Lily Allen boast about their exploits in relation to drinking and sex in much the same way as men. Girl gangs involved in violence and stealing are also becoming more common in the inner cities.

✐ The candidate seems intent on travelling further down the anecdotal road. There is little in this paragraph that is convincing, and the point about girl gangs should be backed up with evidence.

Some sociologists argue that in the contemporary UK, old-fashioned things like class, gender and ethnicity are no longer the main influences on our identity. They argue that people are now more concerned with consuming leisure and making sure they are seen wearing the right logos, drinking the right drinks etc. They believe that women are more interested in stressing these aspects of their lives than stressing the fact that they are women. This new type of femininity therefore means that gender is not used to judge people any more. A good example of this is the dance scene. Thornton points out that males and females who take part in this scene treat each other as equals. It is the music and dancing that is important, rather than trying to attract the opposite sex. Gender is not an issue at these events.

In this paragraph, the candidate becomes more sociologically focused and makes some relevant observations about postmodernism (although the term is not used). The candidate correctly identifies the view that consumption is now allegedly central to modern identity, and links it in a satisfactory manner to changing femininity. The candidate uses an excellent example (the dance scene), and uses a sociological study intelligently to illustrate the general point. However, the inclusion of more studies to support the other points would have been useful.

Feminists still think gender is important, but very few girls call themselves feminists today. If we look at Hey's study, it is doubtful whether the girls in her sample saw themselves as feminist. They were traditional in their attitudes towards boys and sex, and often judged other girls negatively in terms of their looks, bodies etc. It can be concluded that in society today, gender is less important than ever before for identity. New types of femininity and masculinity have appeared, which compete with the idea that women should be mothers and men should be bread-winners. Not everyone agrees with this.

 This is quite a good conclusion, but surprisingly the candidate has elected to conclude that these new types of femininity are dominant, despite the evidence to the contrary (in the form of statistical evidence and sociological studies). The candidate uses the pre-release material well, but despite using Hey as negative evaluation of the essay title, he/she still opts for the optimistic view. Other possible influences, such as social class and ethnicity, are ignored altogether by this candidate.

 **The candidate's answer to part (c) displays some knowledge and under-standing of femininity and associated concepts, but it is largely descriptive. It should also link its existing points more firmly to both traditional and changing forms of femininity. The candidate's major weakness is his/her failure to ground the answer's points in the context of empirical studies — he/she therefore gains 6 marks out of a possible 12 for knowledge and understanding. The range of issues covered is wide, but the response is overly assertive and focused disproportionately on femininity. The candidate therefore gains 4 marks out of 8 for interpretation and analysis. Finally, the candidate uncritically accepts the view embodied in the question and fails to develop any sustained evaluation, gaining 2 out of a possible 4 marks for this skill. In total, the candidate gains 12 out of 24 marks for part (c).**

**(d)** Hey approached a small single-sex school in London and asked for permission to spend time with a group of girls. She attended classes with them, went on cross-country runs with them and spent leisure time with them. She even truanted from school with them. Hey used participant observation in order to find out about their friendships and how girls get on with each other. She wanted the girls to be so used to her presence that they would behave naturally in front of her. She wanted them to trust her in order that they gave her qualitative information that was real. She wanted validity.

📝 This paragraph would benefit from a definition of participant observation. It is unclear which group of girls, in terms of age group, is being observed. The candidate does, however, state how Hey achieved her aim practically of spending time with the girls, and he/she uses concepts such as qualitative and validity confidently.

However, the methods she used to gain their trust can be criticised as unethical. She gave them money and advice. She did not tell the teachers when the girls committed deviant acts, she gave them excuses to miss lessons, and she went truanting with them. However, she says all these unethical things were justified because the girls told her things and behaved in ways in front of her that would not have happened if she had not broken the rules.

📝 This is a satisfactory explanation of Hey's use of ethics.

Hey believed her methods were successful because the girls told her intimate things about themselves and their relationships with other girls and with boys. They were happy to show her notes that had been passed to them in class. She also discovered things that she would never have done if she had just asked the girls to fill in a questionnaire.

📝 This section is vague. There is no discussion about why observation is any better than other methods, such as questionnaires, in terms of obtaining 'intimate things'.

However, I think Hey can be criticised. She only looked at one school in London — this is not very representative. She didn't research many girls, because it was practically impossible to observe more than one small group at any one time. Therefore, she could not generalise from this research.

📝 This is a good point about representativeness and generalisability, but it is under-developed, and could be explored in greater depth and detail.

Second, I don't think the research is reliable. It cannot be checked because it depended on how Hey got on with the girls. We have to take her word on it — it cannot be checked.

📝 This paragraph is repetitive and vague in its explanation of lack of reliability.

Third, the girls might have been flattered by Hey's attention, worked out what she wanted after talking to her and given it to her. It must have been annoying to have this older woman following you about, and I bet they were tempted to lie to her or exaggerate in order to get rid of her. Validity may not be produced by this situation.

📝 These points are valid, but need to be couched in more sociological language, using sociological concepts such as interviewer bias, social desirability and demand characteristics.

Finally, Hey's observations might have been distorted by her feminist beliefs. She might have been overly sympathetic to the behaviour of the girls and critical of anything boys did just because she is a feminist.

*This is a brief, simplistic reference to objectivity.*

**This candidate demonstrates satisfactory, rather than very good, knowledge and understanding of the merits of participant observation and how it relates to Hey's research practices. Unfortunately, the candidate tends to lapse into generalities and overly simplistic language, which undermines the sociological analysis. The range of illustration and use of examples from Hey's work is narrow. Many evaluative opportunities are missed, and the focus is on some of Hey's potential weaknesses rather than on her strengths. This candidate gains 12 marks for knowledge and understanding, 8 marks for interpretation and application, and 12 marks for evaluation and analysis — a total of 32 marks out of a possible 52. This candidate gains 59 marks out of a possible 100 for question 2.**

■ ■ ■

## Answer to question 2: grade-A candidate

**(a)** Historically, the UK was made up of people from a white British ethnic background. However, migration into the UK since the 1950s has resulted in cultural diversity. Ethnic minority groups, originally from the Caribbean islands and the Indian subcontinent, are now part of UK society and make up approximately 8% of the British population.

*This paragraph defines cultural diversity accurately, using detailed historical illustration.*

Cultural diversity has led to the promotion of multiculturalism — the policy that ethnic minority culture should be accepted and celebrated alongside mainstream white culture, and that problems which create racial inequality and tension (e.g. prejudice and discrimination) should be addressed positively. However, there is some evidence from Modood's survey of ethnic minorities that cultural diversity isn't working that well. He found that only a small number of second-generation African-Caribbeans and Asians identified as British, because they felt that the majority of white people did not accept them as such.

**This paragraph links cultural diversity with the related important concept of multiculturalism, which is illustrated convincingly in-depth. The reference to Modood's study is excellent. The candidate gains the full 8 marks for a response of this quality.**

**(b)** First, the workplace was an influential source of identity for traditional manual workers such as miners and factory workers. Billington argues that this was because of the dangerous nature of some of these jobs, e.g. miners depended on each other for mutual safety. The collective nature of factory work — thousands of workers labouring alongside each other, controlled by a minority of supervisors, managers and employers — also contributed to a strong sense of common cause. Billington notes that these factors often led to manual workers seeing the world in a black-and-white, political way, which was marked by conflict between 'bosses and workers' etc. British industrial relations therefore were often underpinned by mutual hostility between management and workers. Most workers belonged to trade unions which militantly pursued workers' interests. The manual working class also voted for the Labour Party, because this was seen as the political party which best supported the interests of workers.

✍ This is an excellent paragraph underpinned by a sociological study that clearly describes and explains the relationship between the workplace and traditional working-class identity.

Another important agent of socialisation was the mass media, especially tabloid newspapers, which were traditionally read by manual workers. For example, the *Daily Mirror* was regarded as a socialist newspaper that always supported the Labour Party in general elections. However, most tabloid newspapers support the Conservative Party. Marxist sociologists have argued that such newspapers have contributed to the decline of the traditional working class because they have encouraged manual workers to see materialism, consumerism, celebrity culture and sport as more important than political issues. Marxists argue that, as a result of this ruling-class ideology, the working class have become more individualistic and the collectivistic and politicised traditional working-class identity has consequently become rare.

✍ **This is a sophisticated paragraph in terms of its theoretical context. However, although the references to Marxism are generally very good, the question itself is focused on how the traditional working class is shaped, so it can be argued that only the section on the *Daily Mirror* is centrally relevant and deserving of reward. Overall, this answer is excellent and the candidate gains 10 out of 12 marks for knowledge and understanding, and 3 marks for interpretation and application.**

(c) In order to assess the view that the dominant values and norms associated with femininity today are very different from those held by previous generations, we need to identify how femininity has been traditionally viewed in the UK. Traditional expectations regarding gender behaviour have resulted in gender stereotyping of female roles. For example, females have been traditionally portrayed as existing in two parallel, gendered universes. The first is the private sphere of the home and family, in which Tunstall notes women are seen as best suited to the roles of domestic goddess, home-maker, wife, romantic, shopper-consumer, mother and emotional caretaker. The second stereotype views certain types of women as primarily sexual beings. Sociologists including Wolf have observed that cultural institutions such as the media are engaged in the sexual objectification of women's bodies, reducing them to dizzy blondes, bimbos and a collection of body parts readily available to men.

This section focuses correctly on what came before the newly emerging forms of gender. It shows an intelligent grasp of concepts and uses examples and studies in an applied and convincing fashion.

Many sociologists have argued in recent years that these stereotypes have come under sustained attack because of economic and cultural changes that have occurred over the last few decades. In particular, UK society has experienced a feminisation of the labour force and economy. Traditional manual jobs dominated by males have gone into decline, resulting in high rates of male unemployment, while the majority of new jobs created have gone to women. Moreover, females have also enjoyed unprecedented educational success in recent decades. It is therefore believed that women have acquired both economic and cultural power. They no longer have to be economically dependent on a male breadwinner.

The candidate provides a full explanation for newly emerging gender roles, underpinned by a reasonably good knowledge of economic and social trends which have benefited females.

It is claimed that such economic trends have led to cultural changes. For example, Sharpe found that when she repeated her classic research of working-class girls, 'Just Like a Girl', in the mid-1990s, girls no longer saw marriage and children as a priority. Careers and economic independence from men were their main goals. Helen Wilkinson, in her 'genderquake' research, argues that young females today are ambitious for careers and are no longer content to follow traditional paths into femininity. In addition, they demand more from men and marriage and are happy to use divorce as a means of escape from an unhappy marriage. They are no longer willing to tolerate empty-shell marriages, abusive men or those unwilling to share the domestic burden. Chandler notes that such women are opting to live in single-person households while they develop their career and independence from men.

This is a sociologically focused paragraph that answers the question by using a range of sociological studies in a perceptive and focused way.

Sociologists have argued that the feminisation of the labour force means men have taken on more emotional caring roles, especially in regard to childcare. There is no doubt that men are more involved, e.g. more men than ever attend the birth of their children. However, it is probably an exaggeration to talk about a 'new man' in touch with his feminine side. Countless studies of the domestic division of labour suggest that women who work outside the home still have the lion's share of childcare, housework and the emotional maintenance of the household.

This is an evaluative paragraph, which intelligently questions the notion that new masculinities and femininities are appearing.

questions & answers

Studies of girls in school also suggest we should not exaggerate the view that females are undergoing a feminist revolution of the mind and are insisting on equal rights with males. Hey's study shows that working-class girls are still traditional in the way they behave around boys and other girls. Many of the girls in her study realised they could control boys using their bodies and the promise of sex. They also negatively labelled and bullied other girls who they felt did not conform to their definitions of what constituted sexiness or good looks. Feminists would argue that such girls are conforming to male patriarchal definitions of femininity. This is similar to the representations of females seen in lads' magazines, which stress the sexual availability of women and judge and label them on the basis of their sexual attraction to males.

🖉 This is an excellent section, which uses the pre-release material well as a means of evaluating the validity of the view contained in the question.

In conclusion, there is no doubt that femininity today is very different from that of previous generations. However, traditional ideas about masculinity and femininity are still widely held by both women and men. Femininity has not displaced masculinity as the dominant gender role. Despite progress in the economy, the Equal Opportunities Commission points out that women are still paid 18% less than men, are still denied access to top jobs, and are still mainly responsible for the family. As Delamont argues, although there has been a great shift in attitudes towards careers and motherhood, the economic system with its glass ceiling, its inequalities in pay and its discrimination against mothers still benefits men at the expense of women. Furthermore, women still bear the bulk of responsibility for childcare even when working in high-powered careers. There is little evidence that the attitudes and practices of men with regard to paid work and family roles have changed dramatically. Changes in attitude and aspiration therefore do not necessarily mean changes in practice.

🖉 The candidate provides an evaluative conclusion that demonstrates a perceptive grasp of the key points, uses key sociological studies and focuses clearly on the issues embodied in the question.

🖉 **This answer to part (c) is a good example of the types of skill required for success at AS. It gains 12 marks for knowledge and understanding, 8 marks for interpretation and analysis and 4 marks for evaluation, making a full 24 marks.**

**(d)** Participant observation is an interpretivist method that involves the sociologist immersing him/herself in the lifestyle of the group being studied. The sociologist participates in the activities of the group being researched and observes its everyday lives. The aim is to understand what is happening from the point of view of those involved, to get inside their heads and understand their interpretation of reality.

🖉 This candidate puts Hey's work into a theoretical context immediately and summarises confidently the rationale for taking this theoretical approach.

Hey used participant observation because she wanted to get insight into the emotional dynamics that characterise the social networks of young females at school. She particularly wanted to investigate how they use talking and writing in their private and intimate relationships and how they coped with male repression. She felt that participant observation was more likely to produce valid data than interviews or questionnaires because it gave her the opportunity to build up a greater degree of trust and rapport with the girls taking part in her study.

✐ This is an excellent justification for the use of participant observation, which links clearly to Hey's aims.

Successful participant observation depends on gaining entry to a group and being accepted by it. Generally, researchers need to share the social characteristics of the group being studied. However, although Hey had the advantage of being female, she was significantly older than the girls being studied. She was also an ex-teacher, which may have aroused suspicion and even hostility.

✐ The candidate successfully and convincingly anticipates problems that might have arisen because of Hey's social characteristics.

There are also ethical problems. There are no clues in the pre-release material, but I assume that Hey had received permission from the local authority, headteacher and parents to carry out the investigation. She initially found that the girls reacted with ridicule or embarrassment when she involved herself in their activities — attending lessons, going on cross-country runs, spending free time with them etc. However, in order to generate trust and valid data, she also engaged in unethical activities — she truanted with some of them. Girls tested her to see if she would report misbehaviour, but she did not do so, in order to earn their trust. She admits openly that she 'traded' with the girls — she gave them gifts of time, money, excuses to miss lessons, attention, advice etc. in return for the girls explaining the motives for their behaviour. She argues that this ethical compromise was necessary, and was justified by the rich, intimate information that she received from the girls.

✐ This is an excellent discussion of the ethical dimension of Hey's research.

There is no doubt that, if the researcher can forge good relations with the group, he/she will see events through the eyes and actions of those being studied. There is some evidence that Hey accessed the interpretations of some of the girls and was able to see their friendship networks through their eyes. For example, the girls explained slang to her and the social context in which friendships were constructed. Most importantly, she was able to use these data to modify her research as she went along. She changed the direction of the research as she observed significant events or as she developed new insights as a result of talking to the girls. Observation is therefore high in validity because Hey could see what the girls did, as opposed to what they said they did when answering an interview or questionnaire.

*questions & answers*

📝 This is a good discussion of the merits of Hey's use of participant observation.

However, on the negative side, the reliability of Hey's research can be questioned, as there is no way to repeat the research and verify her findings. Because friendships were involved, Hey might have lost her emotional detachment or objectivity and consequently been too sympathetic or biased towards the girls in her study. The observer effect is also a problem — we have no way of knowing if the girls played up to Hey's presence and whether they deliberately exaggerated their behaviour. The exchange of gifts may have also produced artificial behaviour — perhaps the promise of money produced unnatural behaviour? Hey could also be accused of abusing friendships — an older woman offering gifts or incentives to young girls seems problematic.

📝 This balanced and detailed analysis and evaluation of Hey's methods is excellent, although candidates should avoid asking questions in examination answers.

We also need to ask how representative Hey's research was. It was confined to one small, single-sex school in London and to young white girls. Asian and black girls were not accessible because of Hey's social characteristics. Only a small number of girls could be observed at any one time, and therefore it is not possible to generalise to other girls on the basis of this study. At best, it is a case study of one set of girls in a London school.

📝 Representativeness is discussed clearly and confidently.

Hey also used a type of secondary data. She regarded the notes that the girls passed to each other in class as symbolic of their intimate emotional relationships. Such notes are documentary forms of evidence — they are a type of expressive document, and according to Hey provided qualitative data about the girls' friendships. As her observation progressed, and as the girls trusted her increasingly, she was given notes that had been passed between the girls. However, we have to be aware that some of these notes might have been written as a direct result of the research — for example, to impress Hey. They may therefore lack validity. It is also possible that Hey misinterpreted their content, and applied meaning to them that was not intended by their authors.

📝 The candidate recognises that Hey went beyond using participant observation. However, this part of the answer is superfluous, because the question only asks the candidate to consider observation.

Overall, Hey's use of participant observation and expressive documents probably produced rich valid data that were unobtainable using other methods — they therefore increased our insight into girls' intimate friendship networks. However, Hey's research also raises questions about reliability, objectivity and representativeness.

📝 This conclusion is a good summary of the contents of the answer — if you have the time, it is always worth summarising your response because it reminds the examiner of the arguments that you have made.

**Overall this candidate demonstrates an excellent knowledge and under-standing of the merits of participant observation, and applies them confidently to Hey's research. A good range of illustrative material is used throughout and a confident use of concepts is consistently demon-strated. Evaluation of ethics and participant observation is sociologically insightful, and of a high standard. However, in his/her enthusiasm for the subject, this candidate gives the examiner more than the question requires. In exam conditions, this could distract the candidate from focusing on the central question of participant observation. The candidate gains 18 marks for knowledge and understanding, 10 for inter-pretation and application and 18 for evaluation and analysis — a total of 46 marks. The candidate therefore gains a total of 91 marks out of a possible 100 for question 2.**

# The formation and meaning of ethnic identities

**Pre-release material: Jacobson, J. (1998)** *Islam In Transition: Religion and Identity Among British Pakistani Youth*, **Routledge**

The aim of this book was to explore the importance of religion in shaping the identities of young British Pakistanis. In particular, Jacobson was interested in why Islam was an exception to the general pattern of religious decline in the UK. She chose to study British Pakistanis because they are the largest Muslim group in the UK. She chose to study young people because she wanted to study the second generation, those who had been born and raised in Britain — and therefore in an environment in which Islam was a minority religion. Moreover, the second generation had also experienced 'identity options' — choices between different sources of identity and Jacobson was interested in why they had opted to choose Islam.

The study was carried out over a period of a year in 1992–93 and took place in the Waltham Forest borough in the East End of London. Waltham Forest was chosen because of its large Pakistani population and because that population is broadly representative of British Pakistanis in general in terms of its age structure and socio-economic status.

The main research method was semi-structured interviews. Respondents were identified using snowball sampling. The interviews which mainly produced qualitative data were conducted with 33 young British Pakistani, 18 female and 15 male. All were aged between 17 and 27, and over a half of them were under 20. Three of the boys and three of the girls were married and one of either sex had children. These 'core respondents' included four pairs of siblings, and so they were from 29 different families. Each interview lasted between an hour and two and a half hours. Jacobson used an interview schedule that contained questions covering the main concerns of the research; religion, identity and family and community. All of the interviews were tape-recorded and transcribed, and extracts from them are used throughout the research to illustrate Jacobson's data. She also supplies details of the socio-economic and educational background of those taking part in the interviews.

Before starting the interviews, she carried out a pilot study with students in order to identify problems and to find appropriate and sensitive ways of asking for the information she wanted.

Jacobson also used three additional research methods. First, she interviewed 30 other respondents informally. These were young people from the British Pakistani community in Waltham Forest and from the wider Asian or Muslim population; for example, she made notes of conversations with young men selling Islamic literature at social events. Second, she observed the life of the community through living there during the period of the research. For example, she visited a large number of social events and activities and approached many community organisations. Third, she discussed with 18 local 'community leaders' their views on the concerns of the research and about the younger generation. These supplementary methods enabled her to gain a greater understanding of how the ideas about identity she heard in the main interviews translated into everyday social life. They also gave her considerable insight into the life of the Pakistani community.

Jacobson found that ethnicity is a difficult area of identity for young British Pakistanis. They have mixed feelings about seeing themselves as British because they are aware that for many people British means being white and having a British heritage. They feel they are bound to their parents' culture and to other Pakistanis; Pakistani ethnicity seems to be something they cannot escape from.

Religious identity, however, was seen differently. Being a Muslim involved choice and was seen as something based on reflection, determination and education rather than something they were born into. She found a very strong social boundary between Muslims and non-Muslims, arising from the nature of Islamic thought and the way it provides clear rules for how Muslims should live. She concluded that Islam provides certainties for young people who face much uncertainty in other parts of their lives — in particular, it involved identifying with a global community unlike Asian or Pakistani identity.

Jacobson's respondents behaved in ways which reinforced the distinctiveness of their Muslim identity. This meant that even when they mixed with non-Muslims, they kept what Jacobson calls 'psychological distance' and they avoided un-Islamic styles of behaviour such as dating and going to nightclubs. However, this did not mean that they retreated into an exclusively Muslim world. The respondents expected and wanted to work, study and socialise outside as well as inside Muslim circles.

(a) **Define the concept of cultural values. Illustrate your answer with examples.** (8 marks)

(b) **Outline and explain how any two agents of socialisation contribute to age divisions and identities.** (16 marks)

(c) **Explain and briefly evaluate why ethnic minority youth in the UK may adopt dual identities.** (24 marks)

**(d)** Using the pre-release material and your wider sociological knowledge, explain the use of observation and interviews to research the identity of young **British Pakistanis**.                                                   (52 marks)

■ ■ ■

## Answer to question 3: grade-C candidate

**(a)** Cultural values are an important part of culture — the way of life of a particular society. Values are widely accepted beliefs that some things are important, such as respect for human life. This value means that the UK has abolished capital punishment, and that, according to the law, murder is unacceptable and punishable by life in prison. We also follow rules when we drive in order to protect lives.

> 🖉 **The definition of cultural values is good and the candidate illustrates it using some good examples. However, these examples should be explored in more detail in order to make explicit how they relate to social behaviour, e.g. it is unclear how following rules when we drive protects lives. The candidate therefore gains 5 marks for knowledge and understanding.**

**(b)** First, the family contributes to age divisions and identities because it teaches children to be dependent on their parents. We live in a society in which children are not encouraged to be independent until the age of 18. The government also encourages parents to protect children, and punishes those who do not conform to the laws which control the behaviour of children, e.g. parents have to send children aged 5–16 to school, and if they do not, they can be fined and imprisoned.

> 🖉 This is a fair point, but the candidate should make up his/her mind whether to focus on the family or the government as the agency of socialisation.

Second, the media contribute to age divisions and identities because newspapers and television convince the older generation that young people are nothing but trouble. Virtually all moral panics in the last 30 years have been about younger people, who are labelled as potentially violent or criminal. This puts pressure on the police, the courts and the government to crack down on young people who might be dressed in ways that the media disapprove of, e.g. hoodies.

> 🖉 **This candidate demonstrates credible sociological knowledge about the mass media and the concepts of moral panics. However, no sociological studies are cited and there are no detailed examples to illustrate how moral panics come about and are sustained. The candidate gains 7 marks out of a possible 12 for knowledge and understanding, but only 2 marks for interpretation and application.**

**(c)** The idea of a 'dual identity' is applied mainly to Asian people and refers to the idea that young Asians exist in two separate worlds. For example, their family and community may demand respect for traditional ways of doing things and for religious values. However, when they are at school or college, and with their white peers, they may act in ways that would be met with disapproval by their elders. They might be loud and aggressive, swear, talk openly about sex and flirt with members of the opposite sex.

🖉 This is a promising opening paragraph that successfully summarises the notion of a dual identity.

The first sociologist to mention dual identity was the Indian sociologist Johal in the 1990s. He noted that third-generation Indians were more likely than their parents to take up Western forms of dress and leisure activities. They were less likely to talk in their mother tongue, except when in the company of their parents and elders. They, especially females, had Western ambitions in regard to education and careers. The film *Bend It Like Beckham* shows a Sikh girl who wants to be a footballer, in the face of opposition from her parents.

🖉 The reference to Johal is excellent, although brief. The reference to the film is not so successful because it is not sociological, and it does not put the film into the context of dual identity.

However, some sociologists, especially Butler and Modood, believe that a dual identity is not always possible for all members of ethnic minority cultures. Butler notes that a dual identity is especially difficult for females, particularly those of Pakistani and Bangladeshi origins, which usually means that they have been brought up in a strong Islamic value system in which females are expected to be passive. They may therefore be denied access to education and careers in favour of marriage and domesticity. Butler notes that middle-class Asian women are more likely to have a dual identity than working-class Asian women.

🖉 There is some confident evaluation of the concept of dual identity using relevant sociological studies in this paragraph. It is a shame that the last sentence is so vague.

Finally, there is evidence from Modood that the idea of a dual identity for many young Asians is temporary, because most eventually conform to a traditional cultural and religious identity. Jacobson identifies a group of young Muslims who she claims reject the idea of a dual identity outright. This is because they believe that Islamic identity should shape all areas of their life and that any Western-style behaviour is sinful and wrong. They therefore see having a dual identity as un-Islamic.

🖉 This is an excellent paragraph which makes some good evaluative points.

🖉 **Overall, this response is quite good, but it is unbalanced, and needs greater demonstration of knowledge and understanding of studies that focus specifically on dual identity. However, this candidate is stronger evaluating the concept and uses sociological studies well to do this. The candidate gains 8 marks for knowledge and understanding, 5 marks for**

**interpretation and application and 3 marks for evaluation and analysis
— a total of 16 marks out of 24.**

**(d)** Jacobson studied British-born Pakistanis to find out what influenced their identity, by using semi-structured interviews. She sampled 33 young people aged 17–27. They were selected by snowball sampling — she asked people who took part in her research to recommend others who would be willing to be interviewed.

*🖉 This is a good introduction, which clearly describes Jacobson's methodology.*

Snowball sampling can be biased, because it is not random. Some sociologists believe that a sample can only be truly representative if it is randomly selected using either systematic or stratified techniques. The danger with snowball sampling is that it results in a biased sample, because people choose others similar to themselves, whose social characteristics may not be typical of the whole population. Jacobson claimed that she overcame this by choosing her sample from one area — Waltham Forest — which is home to Pakistani people similar to Pakistanis in other parts of the country.

*🖉 This is a good evaluation of snowball sampling, as are the references to random sampling.*

Jacobson used semi-structured interviews to question her respondents about religion, family and community. These produced a lot of statistical information and a lot of qualitative stuff. She used extracts from the conversations to illustrate her conclusions. This lets people speak for themselves, and is regarded as increasing validity.

*🖉 Unfortunately this paragraph is vague — the candidate does not explain why semi-structured interviews produce what they do or why people speaking for themselves increases validity.*

She also made the interviews very flexible — they lasted a long time because she wanted people to feel comfortable talking about themselves and their lives. She wanted them to feel that she was genuinely interested in them and for them to tell her things they wouldn't say in an ordinary interview or in response to a questionnaire.

*🖉 Some satisfactory points are raised here but they should be made more sociologically relevant through reference to sociological concepts.*

However, I think her research design suffers from problems. First, she was a woman and the male interviewees might not have wanted to tell her how they really felt, because Muslim men do not tend to regard women as their equals. They might have patronised her or simply not have told her stuff. Second, she wasn't a Muslim either — she says in her findings that Muslims don't really trust non-Muslims, so why should they have trusted her? It is doubtful whether they would have told her how they really feel, especially if they disliked non-Muslims.

🖉 There is some good evaluation here with regard to interview effect, but it lacks a sociological context. It sounds generalised and anecdotal.

Some people might have wanted to give a good impression of themselves. This is called the social desirability effect and is the result of the fact that most people aim to please and ensure that others, especially researchers, think well of them.

🖉 This is a good reference to the social desirability effect, but it would benefit the candidate more to link this to the concept of validity.

Some people might have been suspicious of Jacobson's motives and not given her the full picture, in case she used it against the Islamic community. She did use observation to back up the interview material, but apart from visiting events, it is unclear how this was managed.

🖉 The question clearly asks the candidate to examine the contribution of observation to the overall research, but he/she does not really do this.

🖉 **The candidate has a reasonable knowledge of the merits of interviews and consistently attempts to apply this to Jacobson's research. However, the question also asks for analysis of Jacobson's use of observation, and the candidate generally ignores this. The range of illustrative material used is not bad, but much potential sociological material in the pre-release materials is ignored. The candidate's evaluation of interviews is satisfactory. He/she gains 13 marks for knowledge and understanding, 7 marks for interpretation and application and 13 marks for evaluation and analysis — a total of 33 marks. Overall this candidate gains 63 marks out of 100 for question 3.**

■ ■ ■

## Answer to question 3: grade-A candidate

(a) Values are beliefs and goals that most members of society agree are essential to the smooth and effective running of society. They are an important part of culture because they provide the guidelines on what is morally important and desirable in terms of norms of behaviour. For example, an important value in the UK is respect for human life. This value shapes our behaviour towards others — most of us would not dream of taking another person's life and believe that those who do deserve punishment by the law.

However, values do not remain the same. They are relative to historical periods, societies and subcultures. For example, 50 years ago, the belief that marriage was the only worthwhile context for sexual relationships was dominant because values were shaped mainly by Christianity. However, Christianity today is in decline and some sociologists have observed that sex before marriage and cohabitation are the norm because marriage as a goal has decreased in value.

> *⏎* **This is a focused and detailed definition, which explicitly defines the concept and uses other concepts, e.g. norms, culture and moral guidelines, to illustrate how values are put into practice. The illustration is developed to show the relativity of the concept and applied intelligently to the example of marriage. The candidate gains the full 8 marks.**

**(b)** The mass media are a major contributor to how age divisions are created in the modern UK. There is evidence that the mass media of the 1950s, in the form of the music, film, television and advertising industries, were partly responsible for the creation of adolescent youth culture and, in particular, the concept of the 'teenager'. Commentators such as Savage point out that, before the 1950s, teenagers were not recognised as a separate social category because they were generally no different from their parents in terms of values, tastes, behaviour, dress etc. However, full employment in the 1950s brought about an increase in teenage spending power, and according to Abrams businesses responded to this lucrative new market by developing media products like comics, magazines, pop records and radio stations specifically for the teenage market.

> *⏎* This is an excellent summary of how the 'teenager' was socially constructed. Convincing use is made of sociological studies.

However, there was a negative side to the media construction of the teenager — young people's increasing economic and cultural power was interpreted by members of the older generation as a threat to their authority. Studies by Young, Cohen, Thornton and others suggest that media moral panics were the older establishment's response to this perceived threat. Sensationalist and exaggerated reporting of young people's behaviour created negative stereotypes, or 'folk devils', and resulted in official clampdowns on the young.

> *⏎* The role of the media in the construction of age divisions is further developed through this excellent reference to moral panics.

Another important agent of socialisation with regard to age divisions is the economy, and specifically the workplace. There is evidence that the workplace is an ageist institution — people are required to retire at the age of 65. Arber and Ginn are critical of this because it labels the elderly as essentially useless and dependent, which can lead to the construction of derogatory and abusive labels that marginalise the elderly as inferior to anybody younger than themselves. They are often labelled as a financial and social burden on the rest of society.

> *⏎* **This section is not as convincing as the previous one on youth, because it can be argued that other agencies of socialisation, such as the law or government, are just as responsible as the workplace for ageism against the elderly. However, the candidate makes some excellent sociological observations and uses Arber and Ginn well. The candidate therefore gains 11 marks for knowledge and understanding and 4 marks for interpretation and application.**

**(c)** Dual identities are sometimes called hybrid identities, and refer to ethnic minority youth who feel that they should be loyal to the traditional culture of their parents when they are at home but who also act in Western or British ways when they are in the company of their white peers at school, college, work and in some leisure situations.

*This is a good, succinct definition of the concept, linked to hybrid identity.*

Ghumann argues that Asian children in particular are taught by their parents to believe in traditional values. For example, they are brought up to be obedient to and respectful of their elders and the community. They are taught that the family and community come before the individual and that family honour depends on this.

*The candidate realises the need to contextualise dual identity by discussing how one element of it — tradition — is an important part of family socialisation. The candidate demonstrates good knowledge and understanding of a sociological study.*

Modood found that religion is also important, particularly for children from Pakistani and Bangladeshi backgrounds. Islamic values may shape young people's identity in terms of how they dress, what they eat, how they spend their leisure time etc. For example, Islamic culture may socialise children into accepting that they should marry only someone of their religion, that children should be educated in the teachings of the Qu'ran and that girls should be controlled closely, especially with regard to their contact with males. Girls may also find that they are encouraged to take on domestic responsibilities and marriage rather than higher education and careers.

*This is an excellent summary of the role of religion in socialising children into traditional values, underpinned by a sociological study.*

Butler's study of third-generation Muslim women found evidence that such girls may balance the demands of the traditional and the opportunities offered by education by adopting a dual identity. Many of the girls in her sample adopted Western ideas about education, professional careers and equality, but showed respect for traditional religious ideas by wearing the hijab.

*This is a good use of Butler to introduce the concept of a dual identity.*

Johal focused on second- and third-generation Indian youth and discovered that they saw themselves as having a dual identity — they had inherited a traditional Asian identity but wore a 'white mask' while socialising with their white or African-Caribbean peers at college, work and in leisure time. Swale referred to this as a 'pick and mix' approach — young, middle-class Asians selected what they liked from both British and Asian culture. For example, Asian youth spoke to each other in a language that often combined English and the traditional mother tongue in the same sentence, dressed in traditional dress with Western designs, e.g. the hijab with the Versace logo, and enjoyed music that combined Asian melodies with

Western rock and hip hop. Ghumann referred to dual identities as compartmentalism, although he noted that for girls, the traditional often succeeds in gaining dominance over Western influences, as many girls give up their educational and career ambitions to conform to parental pressures to become a good wife and mother.

🖉 This paragraph uses sociological studies well — Johal and Ghumann, in particular — to illustrate the concept of modern dual identities, or compartmentalism, among young Indians.

Modood argued that dual identities are most likely to be held by middle-class Asian youth. This is because middle-class Asian households are less influenced by religious values. However, as Modood pointed out, the overwhelming majority of Asian youth comes from working-class poorer families, in which religious values are more in evidence. Consequently, most Asian youth return to the collectivistic value system that they learn in childhood. Most choose to organise their domestic and personal lives on the basis of traditional values such as obligation, duty and honour, rather than on Western values. Dual identity is therefore less likely in these cases.

🖉 This paragraph makes some excellent evaluative points with regard to the influence of social class.

Jacobson noted that the traditional is the main shaper of identity for some young Pakistanis. These youth resist the notion of a dual identity, because they reject both British and US culture as immoral and racist. Consequently, they believe in strong boundaries between Muslims and non-Muslims in terms of how they should conduct their lives. They keep a psychological distance from non-Muslims, although they work alongside them in college and in the workplace. Jacobson also found that this group was less likely than other Asian groups to identify with being British — its members were more likely to identify with the global community of Muslims.

🖉 This is an excellent use of the pre-release material. Don't ignore this material — it will generally be useful for any part (c) response you are asked to write.

It is not only Muslims who may have a dual identity. The fastest growing ethnic minority group of children in the UK are dual-heritage or mixed-race children born to white mothers and African-Caribbean fathers (or vice versa). Tizard and Phoenix found that they often faced problems of self-identity because of their experience of racism from black and white communities. These children are likely to see themselves as having a dual identity as a result.

🖉 This is another excellent demonstration of knowledge and evaluation — the candidate acknowledges the need to focus on ethnic groups other than Asians.

Finally, there is a postmodernist view that we all subscribe to a form of dual identity regardless of our social or ethnic backgrounds, because in modern societies the traditional sources of identity — social class, gender, ethnicity, religion and nation-ality — are increasingly being replaced with a wider set of choices underpinned by the mass media, popular culture, materialism, consumption and globalisation. For example, a typical British person may demonstrate his/her dual identity of being British and global by driving a foreign car, by enjoying Indian foods, Australian wines, American music etc. However, sceptics suggest these postmodern arguments are exaggerated.

The candidate constructs an interesting conclusion using postmodernism — it is not convincing, but it demonstrates that he/she is willing to think outside the box.

**This is generally an excellent response. It is focused throughout on dual identity and successfully explores sociological studies on socialisation into traditional values before exploring why dual identities are more likely today than in the past. It also considers issues beyond Asian identity, and the material on postmodernism, which, although not entirely successful, gains some marks. The candidate uses the pre-release material well and is consistently evaluative throughout. The candidate gains 11 marks for knowledge and understanding , 7 marks for inter-pretation and application, and 4 marks for evaluation — a total of 22 marks out of 24.**

**(d)** Jacobson's study aimed to uncover the importance of religion to the identity of second-generation British Pakistanis. She used a range of methods, although the study was mainly interview-based. She wanted to find out why, despite a variety of identity options, some young people of Pakistani origin opted for an Islamic identity.

This is a succinct and accurate introduction to Jacobson's research aims and methods.

Jacobson's main sample was a group of 33 young people aged 17–27 — 18 females and 15 males — living in Waltham Forest, an area that she claimed contained a Pakistani population representative of British Pakistanis as a whole in terms of age ratio, socio-economic status etc. She hoped that by choosing such an area, the people who took part in her research would be a typical cross-section of young Pakistanis, so that she could generalise to other Pakistani communities in the UK.

This paragraph makes a good justification of Jacobson's choice of research sample, with excellent use of concepts.

Her 33 respondents were not chosen by a random sampling method, probably because Jacobson would have had difficulty locating an effective sampling frame. Instead, she used a snowball non-random sampling technique. This usually involves finding and interviewing a person who fits the research needs in terms of their social characteristics and then asking this person to suggest another who might be willing to be interviewed. It is a problematic technique because it does not guarantee a representative sample — most respondents will know each other or belong to similar friendship networks. In Jacobson's case, her initial contacts, who might have had strong Islamic identities, may have introduced her to others with similar outlooks, values etc. A range of typical young Pakistanis — religious, non-religious or less interested in religion — may not have been obtained. The sample she used was probably biased in favour of her hypothesis and research aims.

✍ This is a confident evaluation of snowball sampling, which demonstrates a good knowledge and understanding of sampling in general.

Jacobson mainly used semi-structured interviews to collect her data. These usually have an interview schedule comprising a mixture of closed questions (aimed at collecting quantitative factual information about social backgrounds etc.) and open questions (which give the interviewer flexibility to ask for clarification of vague answers and to follow up interesting responses with additional questions, e.g. by jogging respondents' memories or asking them to give examples). This type of open, flexible questioning is more likely to produce qualitative responses.

✍ This is a good, focused description of semi-structured interviews, which demon-strates a solid understanding of the method.

Interpretivist sociologists are interested in asking open questions because they aim to see the social world through the eyes of those being studied. They are generally interested in how people interpret the world around them, and this was undoubtedly Jacobson's intention. She spent between 1 hour and 2½ hours on each interview — she was looking for depth and detail on issues such as religion, identity, family and community. She tape-recorded each interview and transcribed them. Extracts from the interviews were used to qualitatively illustrate points about how her respondents saw the relationship between religion and identity.

✍ This candidate clearly understands the theoretical rationale underpinning Jacobson's choice of research method.

Her use of qualitative interviewing added to the validity of the study for several reasons. She wanted to make sure her respondents saw that she regarded their interpretation of their religious identity as centrally important to the research. If they felt they were genuinely at the centre of the research, Jacobson thought they would be more likely to open up and say what they really felt and meant. It would reduce their suspicion of her as a woman and a non-Muslim and encourage them to trust her. This rapport would therefore increase the validity of her findings.

✍ This is a good discussion of how the study was characterised by validity.

She also attempted to add data from a number of other angles in order to validate the data from the main sample. She used a form of triangulation by talking infor-mally to 30 other people about Islamic identity and holding discussions with 18 community leaders on religion and identity issues. She also lived in Waltham Forest for the duration of the research and supplemented her interview data with

**question**

observation of young Pakistanis at social events. She probably used multiple methods in order to check or verify the reliability of her interviewing methods and the validity of her findings.

*⚡ The candidate recognises the multi-method approach of Jacobson's research and justifies it successfully.*

Jacobson's research may have experienced some problems. Approximately 73 interviews is not a large sample and, as stated earlier, snowball sampling does not guarantee an objective, unbiased and representative sample from which generalisations can be made to the rest of the young Pakistani population. Jacobson's use of semi-structured interviews may be criticised for lack of reliability because such interviews are often unique — they depend on the relationship between the researcher and subject, making every interview different. The data gained may not be comparable, since the interviewer may have to probe or follow up vague answers in different ways for different respondents. Interviewees therefore might be responding to different questions.

*⚡ The candidate shows a keen evaluative eye and successfully focuses on concepts such as representativeness, comparability and reliability throughout.*

The interview effect is also a problem. Jacobson was white, a woman and a non-Muslim. She may have found that her respondents who admitted to keeping a psychological distance from non-Muslims did the same to her and therefore did not tell her how they really felt about their identity. Some of her respondents may have experienced the social desirability effect and portrayed themselves in the best possible light, which also undermines validity. However, Jacobson was aware of these potential problems and conducted pilot interviews to anticipate and deal with them.

*⚡ The candidate confidently evaluates the problems of the interviewer and social desirability effect when conducting interviews. He/she recognises Jacobson's use of pilot interviews.*

Finally, Jacobson used a form of participant observation, but she failed to consider that her white, female, non-Muslim status might have shaped what people allowed her to see. Reliability is also an issue in her use of observation, because we cannot cross-check what she observed or be sure that what she saw was a correct interpretation of what was actually going on.

*⚡ There is an attempt here to examine Jacobson's use of observation. The candidate makes some pertinent points, but they are brief.*

Overall, Jacobson's study was organised in a multi-method way that probably produced valid qualitative data. However, questions about the reliability of the methodology and representativeness need to be asked.

*⚡ This conclusion is a good attempt to summarise the content of the response.*

🖉 This is an excellent, but unbalanced, response. The question clearly states that candidates should look at both interviews and observation, and although the candidate does make some reference to the latter, the majority of the response is directed at interviews. The candidate demonstrates excellent understanding of the sociological principles that underpin interviews and how these linked to Jacobson's research aims. The range of illustrative material relating to interviews is also impressive, and evaluation is consistently good throughout. However, the failure to assess the role of observation in any depth lets this response down slightly. The candidate gains **17 marks for knowledge and understanding, 10 marks for interpretation and application,** and **17 marks for evaluation and analysis** — a total of **44 marks out of 52.** This candidate gains **89 marks out of 100 for question 3.**

# The formation and meaning of age identities

**Pre-release material: O'Donnell, M. and Sharpe, S. (2000)** *Uncertain Masculinities: Youth, Ethnicity and Class in Contemporary Britain,* **Routledge**

O'Donnell and Sharpe aimed to explore how masculinity is being re-defined and subjected to change in the late twentieth century. They were particularly concerned with the way that young men on the verge of adulthood, especially ethnic minority youth, construct their ideas of what it is to be a man in modern society. They aimed too to explore the variety of different ideas of what masculinity should be like especially with regard to ethnicity and social class. They therefore set out to look at key areas of male lives to discover how boys develop an identity that they can conceive of as masculine. They also investigated the extent to which men find discovering their own male identities problematical and difficult. Finally, they explored the widespread perception that boys are a problem for society.

The research was conducted in the mid-1990s. Questionnaires were completed by 262 boys in four London schools. The boys were aged between 15 and 16 and were generally in Year 11. Three of the schools were in Ealing and one was in the deprived London borough of Hackney. The largest ethnic groups in the study were white, African-Caribbean and Asians, including Sikhs and Muslims. There were a variety of boys from different social classes.

From this initial sample, a further 44 boys were interviewed. Three senior teaching staff were also interviewed. Interviewing techniques would appear to have been largely flexible. In most of the material quoted the interviewer seems to be clarifying the responses of the boys to the line of questioning by simply repeating or rephrasing the previous final statement that the boys had made. The study did not make use of classroom observation and rejected this methodology because they believed that it might lead to the negative labelling of boys and other forms of unfair treatment.

O'Donnell and Sharpe focused on the role of peer groups in the formation of masculine identity. They found that masculinity was important to boys because they wished to dominate social situations. However, many boys were confused about their masculine role because they were receiving mixed messages about it from various sources. For example, school stressed equality and anti-sexism yet the boys still retained sexist and racist attitudes which mainly originated in the home and were reinforced by the media. However, O'Donnell and Sharpe did discover that ideas about masculinity were used as a form of social control. Boys who did not express what were regarded by most boys as the appropriately masculine values and norms were the victims of bullying and homophobia. There was an implicit assumption that sporting types could not be homosexual and that quiet and intelligent boys were prone to homosexuality. Rejection of homosexuality was particularly notable among African and Asian boys.

O'Donnell and Sharpe found that the anxieties and uncertainties boys expressed about masculinity were often the product of the changing nature of the relationship between males and females. The boys expected their futures to be composed of traditional relationships and marriages and were confused and a little insecure when they heard girls being cautious or pessimistic about such relationships. They were particularly confused about balancing being strong, powerful and macho with being sensitive and caring. This was regarded as an uneasy path to tread for a boy. Some boys realised that girls were dismayed by masculine dominant behaviour but this was not enough to put them off crude displays of macho behaviour. This was because the need to display themselves to other males as 'not feminine' was more important. Rejecting female definitions of masculinity as caring and sensitive and being 'laddish' was a defensive reaction to social change and new definitions of what 'being masculine' entails.

They also found that the world of work had changed dramatically for young working-class males. In particular, they found that unskilled manual work was no longer needed and consequently unemployment was high among boys who were not well qualified. Moreover, many new jobs were for females. However, many of the boys in the study expected traditionally male jobs and to take on traditional roles within marriage and the family. Most boys did acknowledge that this would be difficult and that regular employment could no longer be guaranteed. As Tony notes 'My mum and dad say it's not what you want it's what you can get. It's a bit worrying. The unemployment. You have to just get good results and that. If you have no qualifications and that, it's going to be hard'.

O'Donnell and Sharpe note that the collapse of traditional working-class jobs has meant that boys have been forced to contemplate the possible descent into the so-called 'underclass'. There was general agreement, especially among the white and African-Caribbean boys, with the statement 'life is harder for young men nowadays than it has been for their fathers'. They felt that their futures as men were much more uncertain and unpredictable compared with previous generations. There is much greater risk of unemployment and there is unlikely to be a smooth or secure transition into the workforce.

4

**question**

(a) **Define the concept of popular culture. Illustrate your answer with examples.** (8 marks)

(b) **Outline and explain any two ways in which the peer group may influence young people's identity.** (16 marks)

(c) **Explain and briefly evaluate the view that middle-class identity is more strongly developed than working-class identity in the UK today.** (24 marks)

(d) **Using the pre-release material and your wider sociological knowledge, explain the use of questionnaires and interviews to research how the identities of young males are created and reinforced.** (52 marks)

■ ■ ■

## Task

This question is for you to try. You should spend some time researching suitable material and making notes, and then try to write the answer in 90 minutes — the time you will be allowed in the examination. Below are some pointers to get you on the right track.

### Part (a)

You must demonstrate knowledge and understanding in your answer. You should make sure that your definition of popular culture is sufficiently detailed and that you use at least two examples to illustrate your understanding of the concept. These examples could be concrete ones of popular culture in practice, a comparison with high culture or reference to sociological debates and theories that focus on popular culture.

### Part (b)

The focus of this question is on two ways that peer groups socialise young people — these influences may be positive or negative. It is a good idea to begin by making it clear to the examiner what is meant by 'peer group'.

This question rewards you for knowledge and understanding, and interpretation and application. You therefore need to go beyond explanation and use sociological studies if possible, e.g. Sewell on African-Caribbean street subcultures, to illustrate how peer groups may shape the behaviour of young people. You should spend 10–15 minutes on this question.

### Part (c)

All three sociological skills — knowledge and understanding, interpretation and application, and evaluation — are required to answer this question. Begin by explaining what you understand by the term 'middle-class identity', i.e. the identity of the non-manual class of salaried workers which includes professionals, managers, the self-employed and white-collar workers. You could make a number of points with regard to the identity of this group:

- Identify middle-class values and norms that these groups share, e.g. home ownership, suburban lifestyle.

- Note Roberts' argument that this is a fragmentary class.
- Use the work of Savage and others to distinguish differences between, for example, professionals and managers, relating to concepts such as cultural and social capital.
- Explore briefly the proletarianisation thesis of Braverman, who suggested that white-collar workers are more likely to subscribe to a working-class identity today because of profound changes in their work situation.

You also need to explore the concept of working-class identity. This is likely to involve making reference to the following arguments and sociological studies:

- The values and norms that made up the cultural identity of traditional working-class manual workers such as miners, e.g. collectivism, socialism, trade union membership. See Billington and others.
- The decline of traditional manual work due to recession, globalisation, changes in technology and the expansion of the service class.
- The feminisation of the workplace, the genderquake etc. See Wilkinson, Sharpe and others.
- The emergence of a new individualistic and privatised working class. See Goldthorpe and Lockwood, Devine and others.
- The alleged emergence of a poor, casually employed or long-term unemployed, even deviant, underclass. See Charlesworth, Murray and others.
- The pre-release material (O'Donnell and Sharpe) also makes reference to the changing nature of work and the effect of this on the survey population. Don't forget to use this to support the arguments above.

You should aim to spend a maximum of 25 minutes on this part of the question.

## Part (d)
You will receive the pre-release material 2 weeks before your examination. You should familiarise yourself thoroughly with the research methods used and why they were used, i.e. their strengths and advantages. It is important that you refer regularly to the specific research in the pre-release material.

You also need to be aware of the potential weaknesses or disadvantages of the research methods used by the study in the pre-release material. Concepts such as validity, reliability, representativeness, generalisability, sampling, quantitative and qualitative data and objectivity should be used whenever relevant. You should also make some brief reference to positivist or interpretivist perspectives.

The question asks you to use your wider sociological knowledge (of research methods). You must therefore apply in detail your knowledge of the strengths and weaknesses of questionnaires and interviews to O'Donnell and Sharpe's study. Aim to spend about 45 minutes on this part of the question.